Four by Four by Four

Four dangerously entertaining plays

Four performable monologues

Four memorable scenes

For performance, for scene study,
for use as a teaching tool or for use in auditioning

From the white-hot furnace of
Lunchbox Theatre's Petro-Canada Stage One Plays,
a blazing one-act creation machine,
comes a wild and wicked variety of
four one-act plays that feature
monkeys in a rainforest,
a creature returned from the dead,
four wild guys
and one compulsive shopaholic.

Four by Four by Four

Shopaholic
by Glenda Stirling

Monkey Business
by Nicole Zylstra

The Wild Guys
by Andrew Wreggitt & Rebecca Shaw

Borrow Me
by Clem Martini

Edited by Clem Martini

Red Deer P R E S S

PUBLISHED BY
Red Deer Press
A Fitzhenry & Whiteside Company
1512, 1800–4 Street S.W.
Calgary, Alberta, Canada T2S 2S5
www.reddeerpress.com

Edited for the Press by Clem Martini
Text & cover design by Delta Embree & Jacquie Morris, Liverpool, Nova Scotia
Printed and bound in Canada by Friesens for Red Deer Press

Financial support provided by the Canada Council, and the Government of Canada through the Book Publishing Industry Development Program (BPIDP).

 Canada Council   Conseil des Arts   Canadä
for the Arts   du Canada

Library and Archives Canada Cataloguing in Publication
Four by four by four / edited by Clem Martini.
Summary: Shopaholic / Glenda Stirling — Monkey business / Nicole Zylstra —
The wild guys / Andrew Wreggitt & Rebecca Shaw — Borrow me / Clem Martini.
ISBN 978-0-88995-366-6

1. One-act plays, Canadian (English).
2. Canadian drama (English)—21st century. I. Martini, Clem, 1956-

PS8309.U5F68 2008   C812.04108054   C2007-902400-9

United States Cataloguing-in-Publication Data
Martini, Clem, 1956-
Four by four by four / edited by Clem Martini.
[128] p. : col. ill. ; cm.

Summary: Four one-act plays presented to demonstrate the range of the one-act play.
ISBN: 9780889953666 (pbk.)

1. One-act plays, Canadian. I. Title.

812.04108054 dc22 PS627.O53.F68 2008

Contents

Preface

The initial impulse for *Four by Four by Four* arose out of a desire to recognize and celebrate the thirtieth anniversary of Lunchbox Theatre. This tiny, hardworking theatre is, after all, well worth recognizing and celebrating. It is one of the longest-running theatres devoted to one-act plays in North America, and with the inauguration of the Petro-Canada Stage One Plays in 1988 it has become one of the few that has successfully integrated an ongoing new-play development program. Each spring, six new Canadian plays are workshopped and previewed as part of the Stage One program. Of those six plays, nearly half move on to receive professional productions.

These days, two-act plays are the more commonly written and produced form, but the one-act play has a venerable history. This form actually dates back to the festivals of the ancient Greeks, and I am pleased and proud to be associated with an institution that respects and honors those traditions, and at the same time continues to generate new creative work, which renews and re-invigorates the form.

Of course, over the span of nearly two decades of play development, Lunchbox Theatre has spawned a tremendous roster of titles. As a consequence, providing even a sampling represents a daunting task. The four that have been chosen shed a little light upon the kind of aesthetic terrain that has been covered over the years.

The Wild Guys, for instance, is a comedy that examines a theme common in Canadian storytelling—what happens when individuals raised in an urban setting venture into the brooding wilderness? Though the struggles pit man against nature, the discoveries made invariably result in a new and more precise understanding of the human condition. This comedy was a breakout success for Lunchbox Theatre back in 1992 when it premiered. It went on to be adapted as a longer two-act work that proved to be one of the most produced plays in Canada. In its one-act form, however, this play remains a tightly constructed, comic gem.

Shopaholic, a thoroughly urban play, mines humor from what is essentially one woman's tragic yearning for acceptance, security, self-empowerment, and a really great pair of pants. Premiering in 2002, it proved to be a tremendous success with an audience that recognized something strangely familiar in Abby's tragic-comic struggle.

Borrow Me, one of thirteen plays I've had premiered at Lunchbox Theatre, represented a bit of a departure for me at the time it was first produced in 1997. The majority of the plays I'd had produced by Lunchbox had been comedies, but this play mixed genres and bent genders. It can be viewed, alternately, as a drawing-room comedy, an avenger's tale or a bit of a supernatural thriller.

Monkey Business, produced in 2004, is the most recent of the collection, and is essentially a sweet romantic comedy fueled by a frighteningly high IQ. It drops a bright young couple into the steaming jungle and then examines how love can survive this struggle between heavyweight intellects. Fate, self-determination, ageism, evolution and the relationship humans share with the natural world are all thoroughly explored and tested as monkeys crash through the canopy and Horace and Myriam move closer to an understanding and acceptance of their feelings for one another.

Together, these plays provide readers with a rare variety to select from. As a study of Canadian works developed over the past few decades it offers a fascinating survey. As a text to dip into for future production, it should prove extremely useful. There are a nearly equal number of roles for actors of either gender. The plays can easily be produced on the kind of Spartan budget that colleges and community theatres are often compelled to work within. And as an additional benefit, there are four scenes and monologues set aside for in-class study, use as acting exercises, or for employment in auditions.

Lunchbox is moving confidently into its fourth exciting decade. As a complement to that transition, here are four terrific one-act plays, as well as four compelling scenes and monologues, for your study and entertainment.

Enjoy!

Clem Martini

Introduction

Imagine watching Picasso paint. Would it change what he painted? How he painted? What role would the presence of an "audience" play in the ultimate dynamic of his canvas? An audience changes everything. If it didn't we'd spare ourselves the fear, the pressure, the need for absolute clarity, and, of course, the moment of judgment. We'd work in a vacuum . . . like so many of our playwrights have to do.

New play development invites the playwright in from the wilderness. It offers practical resources and fresh influences at critical stages in their work. It builds capacity for the global theatre industry by increasing the number of productive writers. It also enriches the audience's experience.

The Petro-Canada Stage One series is a fundamental part of Lunchbox Theatre's DNA. Created by Bartley Bard in 1988, this new play development program annually commissions six original one-acts by Canadian writers. Many of these scripts go on to premiere at Lunchbox Theatre, to enjoy prosperous lives at theatres around the globe and, sometimes, to find alternate lives as screenplays, television scripts or full-length works. The goal of Stage One is to aid the playwright, enrich the play and involve the public. It appeals to artists and patrons alike. It also produces some fabulous one-acts.

Blaise Pascal once commented on a letter he'd just finished: *"The present letter is a very long one, simply because I had no leisure to make it shorter."* That's the challenge of the one-act. Concision. Precision. Economy.

The four delightful plays in this volume were developed through our Petro-Canada Stage One Plays. The playwrights are dedicated professionals who chose to open their processes rather than protect them, to engage with their colleagues and risk a dialogue with the audience while their ideas were still crystallizing, their words still evolving. They are defined, not only by the high quality of their results and their ability to reach their respective destinations, but by the strength, inclusiveness, and depth of their journeys. Hats off to them, and to their excellent work!

Rona Waddington

The Wild Guys

By
Andrew Wreggitt & Rebecca Shaw

The Wild Guys was commissioned by the Petro-Canada Stage One Plays. The one-act version premiered September 28, 1992 at Lunchbox Theatre, Calgary, with the following cast.

STEWART:	Daryl Shuttleworth
ANDY:	Vince Metcalfe
RANDALL:	Howard Siegel
ROBIN:	David LeReaney

Directed by Margaret Bard

Set Design by Tracy Nunnally

Lighting Design by Steve Isom

Costumes by Hal Kerbes

Stage Manager: Donna Sharpe

The Wild Guys was originally workshopped as part of the Petro-Canada Stage One Plays in May of 1992 with Daryl Shuttleworth (Stewart), Bartley Bard (Andy), Howard Siegel (Randall), and David LeReaney (Robin). The workshop was directed by Margaret Bard.

Characters
STEWART GYVER
ANDY GRAHAM
RANDALL HARRISON
ROBIN CUNNINGHAM

Scene One

Spotlights come up on the head and shoulders of the four wild guys, all of whom are on the telephone. STEWART GYVER is in a grocer's apron. ANDY GRAHAM has a tie and jacket on. RANDALL HARRISON has on a white shirt and tie, askew. ROBIN CUNNINGHAM is wearing a collarless shirt and a leather thong around his neck with an animal claw of some kind dangling from it.

STEWART: Maxie, it's me . . . Listen, good news . . . I got a call from Andy Graham, the guy from head office? . . . No, no, the big honcho who was so impressed with Hawaiian Crazy Daze. He wants me to go with him on a guys' weekend kinda thing. It can only mean he wants to talk promotion . . .

ANDY: Yes, Barbara Graham please. It's Mr. Graham . . . her husband . . . Ask her to step out of her meeting, please.

STEWART: Well, you know, maybe a bigger outlet . . . wouldn't that be somethin'? Life in the big city? . . . I dunno. Airdrie, Wetaskiwin . . . who knows . . .

ANDY: Hi, Barbara, it's me . . . I just wanted to remind you that I'm going on my weekend men's retreat today . . . Well, in that case I probably won't see you before I go. We're driving up tonight and starting out for the lake early tomorrow morning . . . Randall, Robin and a fellow from our store in Lone Pine . . . Yes, the same guy who came up with that bizarre Hawaiian promotion . . .

RANDALL: Hi Tammy . . . Bad news, kitten. I can't make it this weekend . . .! I know I did . . . Tammy, believe me there's nothing in the world I would love more than to do the triathlon with you . . . I know . . . and I feel terrible about it. But I totally forgot that I promised Andy I'd go on this men's sensitivity weekend with him . . .

ROBIN: Mrs. Filbert? . . . Hi there, it's Robin . . .

RANDALL: He's a very important client, a top executive at the Co-op and he's really into that shit . . .

ROBIN: Robin Cunningham from the Eco-Store? . . . Oh, I'm fine dear, how are you? . . . That's a shame . . . uh huh . . . listen the reason I was . . . uh huh . . . I know, what can you do? Cats just go wherever they want to, don't they? Listen, the reason I was calling was I promised I'd sit with you at the recycling bin on Saturday . . . no, no this Saturday. Anyway, I can't make it. This wonderful opportunity has come up. One of the guys from my local men's group is going to take a few of us out on a soul exploration weekend.

STEWART: Aw, you know. Drink a few beers, fish a little. He's bringin' a coupla pals from city.

ROBIN: You know, men rediscovering their primal natures in the forest.

ANDY: What's Danny up to this weekend?

ROBIN: No, the forest, Mrs. Filbert, not the florist . . .

ANDY: Well, maybe you should keep an eye on him . . . Yes, I remember what Linda said about trust . . .

RANDALL: I know it's not very far but there's an older guy coming along.

ANDY: All weekend? Why are you meeting on the weekend? . . .

ROBIN: I know. Bus passes are way too expensive in this city . . . Listen, I've got to go, Mrs. Filbert . . .

STEWART: I know. A few beers, that's all. I gotta go. Bye.

ANDY:	Then I'll see you Sunday night, *after* your meeting. Bye.
RANDALL:	Right. Kisses. Good luck this weekend. Bye.
ROBIN:	OK. Remember, ten to twelve, *this* Saturday. Bye.
ALL:	Jesus!

Blackout. Suggested music bridge: Paul Simon's "Obvious Child" drum intro.

Scene Two

As drumbeats continue, rosy stage lights very slowly fade up, an imitation of the rising sun. Onstage are a few trees and several large rocks suggesting bush country. STEWART enters stage left. He wears a worn and bulging backpack that clinks mysteriously. He is followed by an enthusiastic, but exhausted, ROBIN, whose own extra-large backpack has a deerskin drum and guitar tied to it. Next comes RANDALL, still looking fresh and fit ... then ANDY brings up the rear. The men walk single file across the stage and exit stage right. A long beat. Music fades. STEWART re-enters from stage right, followed by ROBIN, RANDALL, and ANDY. They continue walking toward stage left, in the same single file.

RANDALL:	Hey, uhh . . . Stewart?

STEWART turns and they all stop. ROBIN immediately throws himself down to rest.

RANDALL:	We were just here.
STEWART:	*(looking around, a little confused, then lies)* Yeah. I was gonna take us on a short cut but decided against it.
ROBIN:	Can we rest for a while?
RANDALL:	If it's five miles in to this lake . . . *(checks his watch)* It's been two hours of bushwhacking . . . We should be getting close.
STEWART:	*(still looking around)* Oh, yeah. We're close, very close.

ROBIN: God, it's wonderful, isn't it? I can already feel the primal
            blood starting to course through my veins!

*STEWART is taking off his pack. He looks over at ROBIN a little skeptically.
STEWART's pack clinks as he puts it down.*

ANDY: You know, in Dr. Rothenberg's new book he says that it's
            important to physically remove yourself from the source
            of your stress in order to begin some kind of healing
            process.

ROBIN: That is so true!

RANDALL has been looking around, still wearing his pack.

RANDALL: *(to STEWART)* You'd tell us if you thought you might be
            lost, right?

STEWART: *(laughs a little too heartily)* Lost! We're not lost . . . my
            God, I grew up out here, *(realizes something)* not that I
            wouldn't consider moving. I mean, if the right opportunity
            came up . . .

RANDALL: And this lake, this Zippermouth Lake, you've been there,
            right?

STEWART: Well, not me personally, but I got real clear directions from
            my buddy Rick. The fishing's supposed to be fantastic,
            you know, that's why they call it Zippermouth Lake, only
            about five guys know about it. You don't want lots of people
            makin' a trail in here and fishin' the lake out.

RANDALL: No, we wouldn't want to have a trail to follow.

As ROBIN talks, STEWART starts unloading beer bottles from his pack.

ROBIN: I feel good, you know? Whooo! The city just beats the
            masculinity out of a guy, but out here you can feel the
            warrior standing up in you, the wildman starting to stalk
            back there in the old subconscious . . . You know what
            I'm thinking? I'm thinking why don't we start doing some
            body work? I mean let's get right into it.

STEWART:	*(looking up)* My brother does body work. He has a shop in Red Deer.
ROBIN:	That's not the kind of body work I meant.
STEWART:	Anybody want a beer?
RANDALL:	It's eight-thirty in the morning, Stew.
STEWART:	*(cracking a beer)* Yeah, time's a wastin'.

STEWART offers the beer around but gets no takers. He shrugs and takes a long pull himself.

ROBIN:	I'm talking about physically preparing the body for a spiritual journey. Meditation, Chi self-massage . . . Do you know what I'm talking about?
STEWART:	(snorts) Self-massage . . . yeah, right.
ROBIN:	We do it every week.
STEWART:	Yeah, who doesn't, eh?
ROBIN:	In our group, before every meeting.
STEWART:	You do it . . . together?
ANDY:	Stewart, Robin is talking about a Taoist form of mental and physical relaxation. Like rubbing your kneecap a certain way, or the back of your neck . . .
STEWART:	*(the light comes on)* Ohhh . . .
ANDY:	I'd hoped we could do a full body work session, too, Robin, but maybe we should wait until we get to the cabin . . .
ROBIN:	It's just that the weekend is so short. You know, a little meditation might ease us through the transition we're making as we physically pass from the desensitized world of civilized man to the hyper-sensitive world of forest man.
STEWART:	What?

ANDY: I don't know, Robin. Maybe this isn't the right moment.

ROBIN: Just a quick centering exercise, Andy?

ANDY: Well, if that's all right with everyone else. Randall?

RANDALL: Sure, why not? Maybe "forest man" over there will figure out where we are.

ANDY sits cross-legged on the ground and ROBIN and RANDALL both imitate the position.

ANDY: Stewart, you'll join us, won't you?

STEWART: You know, I thought maybe we'd a have a few beers, a few yuks, you know but like I don't know anything about this stuff you're talkin' about . . .

ROBIN: *(impatiently)* Oh, for heaven's sake. It's meditation. It's not that difficult a concept to grasp . . . it's about using your brain . . .

ANDY: Come on, Stewart, try it. You might be pleasantly surprised by the experience.

STEWART reluctantly assumes the position.

ANDY: OK, everyone, eyes closed . . . Now breathe in deeply . . . and out. Breathe in . . . and out . . .

STEWART: This isn't some sort of weird cult, is it?

ROBIN: Oh, sweet Jesus!

STEWART: . . . 'cause like I'm Presbyterian, eh?

ANDY: No, it's not. Just relax, Stewart. Breathe in . . . Start to feel the earth's energy being drawn up through you . . . and out. You're like a tree with roots . . . up from the center of the earth, through your buttocks and into your lungs and out through the top of your head. Breathe in . . . can you hear the Chi beginning to move in you like a wind, awakening your heart and lungs and liver and . . .

STEWART:	I can hear my stomach.
ROBIN:	Oh, God, this is hopeless!
STEWART:	Well, I'm hungry.
ANDY:	Maybe we should wait until we're at the cabin and we're a little more comfortable with each other. I'm sorry, Stewart, I guess I didn't explain very clearly the nature of this weekend.
STEWART:	No, no, look, I don't want to put a damper on things . . . I'm as hip as the next guy, you know. I just thought when you said a guys' weekend you meant . . . you know . . .
ROBIN:	Drinking and throwing up?
STEWART:	*(tentatively)* Yeah.
ANDY:	It's a different sort of guys' weekend, Stewart. Let me try and explain. A couple of years ago, I realized that my lifestyle had left me isolated, without many real male friends. I had achieved "success" in my personal and professional life, but I still felt that something was missing. I began to attend a regular men's meeting, just a study group really, but I was fascinated by getting to know this diverse new network of men.
STEWART:	Network?
ANDY:	Weekends like this are about men talking to men. Really talking.
STEWART:	You mean about work? Like jobs? Promotions and stuff?
ANDY:	Yes, but not just that. We also talk about how we feel. What drives us, what makes us feel sad, or fulfilled . . .
RANDALL:	Well, I'm with Stewart. What I feel is hungry.
STEWART:	Yeah! I'm starved. Where's those cheezies, Robb?
ROBIN:	My name is not Robb, it's Robin.

STEWART: Right. Whatever. C'mon. Cheezies.

ROBIN doesn't move to open his pack.

RANDALL: Robin . . . all the food's in your pack. Let's go.

ROBIN: *(pause)* Well, I didn't want to spoil the surprise, but I guess I have to. *(beat)* I didn't bring any food.

RANDALL: Ahuh. That's very funny, Robin. Now make with the Cheezies, OK?

ROBIN: Don't you see? This is the perfect way to draw the wildman out of us. We spend a weekend hunting and gathering, like countless generations before have, back to the dawn of time itself.

ANDY: This is something we should have discussed as a group, Robin.

STEWART: Jesus! All I brought was beer!

ROBIN: We can smear the blood of our prey on our faces, become one with the spirits of the forest.

RANDALL: Our prey? I don't know about the rest of you, but when I get hungry, I get cranky.

ROBIN: It's all the stress of your city life. The body work will help with that . . .

RANDALL: I can think of one kind of body work that might help.

RANDALL moves toward ROBIN menacingly.

ROBIN: *(delighted)* See? Already, the primal male aggression is asserting itself. *(he hugs RANDALL)* Whoo! This is gonna be a great weekend!

The stage goes black. Suggested music: "Wild Thing."

Scene Three

Stage lights up to reveal a slightly different arrangement of trees and rocks. The lighting now indicates mid-day. RANDALL, ROBIN and ANDY kneel downstage center, looking over the edge of the stage. Music fades out. RANDALL holds a string over the edge; a safety pin is attached to the end. They are fishing.

ROBIN: *(whispers)* There's a big one!

ANDY: *(whispers)* He's coming closer . . . hold it steady now . . .

ROBIN: Don't you think you should jig it up and down a little?

RANDALL: I will . . . shhh . . . come on you beauty . . . bite that safety pin . . .

STEWART enters stage right, zipping up his fly. He looks around and casually picks up ROBIN's guitar. He thinks for a minute, then aggressively strums it and begins to sing. RANDALL, ROBIN and ANDY leap about a foot in surprise.

STEWART: *(a scratchy howl)* There is a house in New Orleans they call the Rising . . . Uhh . . . sorry.

STEWART notices his audience is not totally enraptured by the song. He puts the guitar down a little guiltily. RANDALL yanks the string back and throws it down petulantly.

RANDALL: Great! We find the one fish in this whole creek and our fearless local guide decides to give a concert.

ROBIN: I know we lost the fish, but look how we were pulling together, striving toward our common cause.

RANDALL: Don't start with that shit, Robin. I'm sick of it. If it hadn't been for you we'd be having a pleasant hike instead of rooting around for something to eat like a gang of yuppie hoboes! On top of that *(points a finger at STEWART)* I don't think he knows where he's going, Andy.

STEWART: Sure I do. We're almost there, *(pause. RANDALL just looks at him)* Honest.

ANDY: I know you're hungry, Randall, but you're reacting in a fairly aggressive manner.

ROBIN: He's so goal-oriented.

RANDALL: *(looks at ROBIN)* It's not as though I haven't been provoked.

ANDY: I'm not criticizing that, Randall. It's natural. It's just that men are often in situations where they have strong feelings but they're required by social convention to hide them. That's one thing this kind of weekend tries to achieve. We try to identify emotions that are riding just below the surface. Anger, grief, fear, loneliness . . .

RANDALL: Look, all I want is a cheeseburger.

ROBIN: *(gleefully)* But you can't have one and that's the point!

ANDY: Look, I'm not a psychologist, but it's something we all grapple with in our own way. The expression of anger has been socialized out of us, but what do we do with that energy?

ROBIN: *(eagerly, over ANDY)* We transfer it.

ANDY: We transfer it.

RANDALL: I think it was a rhetorical question, Robin.

ANDY: Unless we can identify it and deal with it . . .

ROBIN: You say you're angry about the lack of food, but really you're angry at your absent father. You're furious that he didn't initiate you into the world of men, that you were robbed of your mythopoetic heritage . . .

RANDALL: Just shut up, Robin. *(turns to ANDY)* Look, I agreed to come along on this weekend but I'm not crazy about Doctor Freud over here playing clinical psychologist on me.

ROBIN: Still hanging on to that macho resistance . . .

RANDALL:	Especially when Doctor Freud wants to smear blood on his face and dance around a fire.
STEWART:	We're not gonna actually do that, are we?
ANDY:	Randall, you came on this weekend to indulge me, right? Important client, you didn't want to turn me down.
RANDALL:	No, it's not like that.
ANDY:	But you know deep down you wouldn't have lost me as a client. You also came for another reason, didn't you?
RANDALL:	Well, it sounded like this was going to be fun.
ANDY:	But is fun a means or an end?
RANDALL:	Does it matter?
ANDY:	Why did you come?
RANDALL:	OK. My girlfriend wanted me to go on a triathlon.
STEWART:	Jesus, really?
RANDALL:	She's twenty-two. I mean, every weekend it's something else, you know? Ice wall-climbing, mountain biking . . . Shit, a triathlon! All I could think was, "great, there's one I won't have to do." I was looking forward to relaxing and healing up. I was hoping for bacon and eggs, steaks fried in butter, baked potatoes and sour cream . . .
ROBIN:	What is that? Quest for cholesterol?
RANDALL:	Shit, you know, I'm thirty-nine years old. It's tough to hold down a job and keep up with her . . .
ANDY:	Why do you have to keep up?
RANDALL:	Because if I don't, I'll lose her.
ROBIN:	Wait! Wait! I just remembered. *(starts to dig in his pack)* I brought the talking crystal. I went to an anger workshop last year at Mendocino and the talking crystal really helped.

STEWART: A talking crystal?

ROBIN: The idea is, the speaker holds the crystal and as long as he holds it, no one interrupts. Then you pass it on. After a while, I swear the thing gets hot to hold, it's so full of psychic energy.

ANDY: We're already talking, Robin.

ROBIN: Yeah, but we didn't ritualize the space first . . .

ROBIN has gotten the crystal out now; STEWART examines it with curiosity.

STEWART: Whoa! That's some rock!

ANDY: (back to RANDALL) I thought you were seeing someone in your firm.

RANDALL: Judith. Yeah, well, that didn't turn out to be a very good idea. I think we were too similar.

ANDY: In age?

RANDALL: A little below the belt there, Andy.

ANDY: Exactly.

ROBIN: It's a classic. Fear of mortality. You keep getting older but your girlfriends stay the same age.

RANDALL: There's nothing wrong with a little fear of mortality, know what I mean, Robin?

STEWART: *(finally gets it and laughs)* Below the belt. Haw.

ANDY: I understand the stress of the legal profession can be very hard on relationships.

RANDALL: Yuh. Well, maybe we should keep looking for this cabin. So we have a little more time for hunting and gathering.

They all stand up and start to pull on their packs.

STEWART: *(still admiring the crystal)* So where did you find this rock anyway?

ROBIN: Birks.

Stage lights fade to black. Suggested music: "Born To Be Wild" by Steppenwolf.

Scene Four

Stage lights go up. The lighting indicates that it's early evening now. The moveable scenery has been altered again. Music fades down. Enter the four intrepid hikers, filing wearily across the stage in this order: STEWART, ROBIN, ANDY, RANDALL.

ROBIN: *(as he walks)* I can't believe you did that!

RANDALL: Look Robin. He's been saying he's sorry for two hours. Can't you just drop it?

The wild guys file off. Long beat. They come back on in the same order.

ROBIN: Cost me four hundred and fifty bucks.

STEWART stops and the line bumps to a stop behind him.

STEWART: I just put it down, you know, to go take a pee . . .

ROBIN: Oh sure, he puts down a four hundred and fifty dollar crystal on a scree slope.

STEWART: Well, it's a bunch of rocks. They all look the same!

ANDY: We lost a whole hour looking for that crystal. Maybe we could cut our losses here.

STEWART puts his pack down and pulls out another beer.

ROBIN: I had a lot of psychic energy invested in that thing.

RANDALL: *(ready to tear his hair)* It's a rock! A rock! If you paid four hundred and fifty bucks for it, that's your fault! Stop whining! God! I'd go home if I knew where the hell I was!

RANDALL yanks a beer out of STEWART's pack for himself.

ROBIN: *(petulantly)* Robert Bly held that crystal once.

ANDY: Look Robin, Stewart has apologized. Be gracious about it and put it behind you.

RANDALL: *(to STEWART)* You're lost.

STEWART: Am not.

RANDALL: You are too! Admit it!

STEWART: No.

RANDALL: *(to the others)* He's lost. So are we. We don't have any food, we don't have a tent . . .

ROBIN: Or a crystal.

RANDALL: . . . and it's going to be dark soon.

STEWART: Maybe I took us, sorta the long way around but . . . *(RANDALL laughs)* but we're not exactly lost.

RANDALL: How could we be more "exactly" lost? In what possible, hypothetical way could we be more thoroughly or precisely lost? In your opinion.

STEWART: *(looks at ANDY)* He's a lawyer, isn't he?

RANDALL stalks off and looks back the way they came. STEWART looks over at ROBIN who also turns his back.

STEWART: OK. So we're kinda lost. The lake shoulda been back there. I dunno. Rick's directions were a little vague.

ANDY: You didn't feel you could share that with us earlier? When we might have been able to help?

STEWART: Welllll . . . You know . . . I didn't want you guys to think . . .

ROBIN: That you have the wilderness instincts of my neighbor's Shih Tzu?

STEWART: Come on. It's gotta be around here somewhere.

STEWART leads the three others offstage in the same single file. Stage lights go down. Music comes up. "Born To Be Wild."

Scene Five

Stage lights come up. It is sunset. A last red streak on the horizon. STEWART, RANDALL and ANDY sit around a small campfire. Four sleeping bags are stretched out around them. ANDY holds a Tilley Endurables hat, full of berries. Music fades.

RANDALL: It's just I thought the idea was we would pool the berries we picked and then divide them up.

ANDY: And that's what we're doing . . .

RANDALL: Yeah, except Stewart was over there grazing in the bushes like a bull moose.

STEWART: I was not.

RANDALL: Yes, you were. I saw you. Do you do that in your produce section at work? I don't see why we should have to share the berries we picked while he was over there filling his face.

STEWART: I wasn't filling my face.

ANDY: OK. I make out eighty-three Saskatoon berries here. It's not great, but it's the best we could do given the light. So that's twenty berries each.

ANDY counts out his berries, then passes the hat to STEWART, who begins counting out his berries.

RANDALL: Plus one extra for everyone except Stewart.

ANDY: Don't you think this is getting just a little petty?

STEWART: *(He dumps his berries back in the hat and hands it to RANDALL)* Here. They're all yours. Crybaby.

Enter ROBIN. He has a red bandana tied around his head, something that looks like blood smeared on his cheeks, and he carries a sad-looking stick, which he imagines is a spear. He walks energetically towards the campfire, hopping on one foot and then the other, ready to dance around it. After a beat, the others notice him.

RANDALL: What are you doing?

ROBIN: A warrior should celebrate his fire. Yeah! Celebrate the evening feast! Come on, you guys!

STEWART: What've you got all over your face?

ROBIN: The blood of the prey!

RANDALL: Saskatoon berries?

ROBIN: Well, we haven't caught any prey yet. But that's what the books say you're supposed to do . . . Hey, I know, we could build a sweat lodge!

ANDY: Why don't you just sit down and eat your supper, Robin?

RANDALL: Someone forgot to bring his Ritalin.

ROBIN: What kind of warriors are you guys, anyway? I mean, you don't wanna do anything.

RANDALL: You mean other than eat and sleep indoors?

ROBIN: Hey, I lost a very important object today . . . *(the others all groan)* A sacred object . . . but I'm getting through it. I'm ready to try and keep the spirit of the weekend alive. Which is more than I can say for you guys.

ANDY: Robin's right. We shouldn't let these misfortunes stand in the way of our weekend.

ROBIN: When I was at Mendecino, we built a fifteen-foot wooden penis and did a very emotional naming ceremony around it.

RANDALL: Let me guess. You named it Dick.

ROBIN: No. We named each other. But obviously, you guys aren't ready for that kind of breakthrough.

RANDALL: I'm definitely not.

ROBIN: I'm trying to pass on the benefit of my experience, in the tradition of male oral culture.

STEWART: Who wants another beer?

They all accept a beer this time. Even ROBIN.

ROBIN: While you guys were arguing over a handful of Saskatoon berries, I was setting a rabbit snare. In the morning, we'll be roasting rabbit over our breakfast fire.

RANDALL: Where did you learn to set a rabbit snare? *The New York Times* guide to outdoor gastronomy?

ROBIN: "The Weekend Warrior Handbook. New Age edition."

RANDALL: I hope you won't be offended if I don't start sautéing the onions yet. Anyway, bunny breakfast or not, I think we should try and find our way back tomorrow.

STEWART: Go back?

ROBIN: Oh, I see. You're just going to give up.

RANDALL: I'm not giving up. We're lost. I think it would be prudent to make an effort to get home.

STEWART: We can still find the lake tomorrow. It's gotta be around here somewhere.

ROBIN: When the going gets tough, the tough run for their BMW's.

ANDY: I know this was all kind of unexpected but in some ways the real-life challenges of not having food or shelter do present a unique opportunity. It's a well-known fact that a man's true character emerges when he's under pressure. The kind of pampered lives we lead never give us the opportunity to explore that aspect of ourselves. I mean who are we, really?

RANDALL: The four stooges.

ANDY: Now that we've been challenged in a physical way, are we courageous enough, Randall, to look farther and challenge ourselves emotionally?

RANDALL: I'm sorry, Andy, but all this navel-gazing gives me the willies.

ROBIN: You're afraid of what you might find.

RANDALL: Lint, that's all. Look, Hiawatha got us lost and Dr. Freud is trying to starve us to death. My warrior instincts are telling me to go home and order a pizza.

STEWART: Well, I think Andy's right. OK, so I got us lost, we can still make the best of it. We got some beer, it's not raining . . . We can still turn this thing into a successful weekend. Just like I did with Hawaiian Crazy Daze. You remember my Hawaiian Crazy Daze promotion, right Andy?

ANDY: Oh, yes. I remember.

STEWART: Palm trees made outa crepe paper? The checkout girls in the hula skirts? That was all my idea. And talk about moving produce. Hey, we sold one heck of a lotta pineapples.

ANDY: Which was fortunate since you ordered an entire truckload by mistake.

STEWART: Yeah, OK, but we sold most of 'em, right? I mean, it could have been worse. I really think that shows I'm ready for more responsibility.

ROBIN: Maybe, but don't let him carry your crystal, Andy.

STEWART: I've been managing the store in Lone Pine for ten years, now. I feel like I'm ready for a new challenge within the organization. A bigger store maybe.

ANDY: Hawaiian Crazy Daze certainly showed what you're capable of.

STEWART: Thinking on your feet. Adapting to new challenges. That's what it takes to be a good manager, right, Andy?

ANDY: Let's talk business another time, Stewart.

STEWART: Another time. OK! All right! Then let's have some fun! I mean we're on a guys' weekend, right? The old lady isn't here to tell us to mow the lawn or clean up dog pooh. We're free! Come on! Hey, Robb, you brought your guitar. Why don't you give us a tune?

STEWART grabs the guitar and hands it to ROBIN.

ROBIN: *(fake modesty)* Well . . . I don't know . . .

STEWART: I know most of the chords to a few Neil Young songs . . .

ROBIN: *(quickly grabs the guitar from STEWART)* There is one piece I've been working on.

STEWART: Right on! OK, what is it? Dylan?

ROBIN: Actually, it's my own composition.

STEWART: Wow! Great!

ROBIN: I was at Mendecino in May for a combined Encountering Your Inner Shadow and Power Dancing workshop. I was meditating by myself one day when I started watching this bumblebee as it was approaching a flower. It was a beautiful dance of power and yielding. So I wrote this piece. It's called . . . "Encounter."

ROBIN pauses dramatically, then in an overblown way, plinks the strings of the guitar above the bridge. He pauses again, then attacks the bass string, thumping up and down on the same three notes in imitation of a four hundred pound bumblebee. Pause. Plink. Thump. Repeat until nauseated. ROBIN ends his song with a flourish. There is a long empty pause.

STEWART: Do you know any Creedence?

RANDALL: That's the stupidest thing I've ever heard.

ROBIN: Well, I can see that some of us aren't courageous enough to be emotionally challenged tonight.

ANDY: That was very interesting, Robin. You know, Robert Bly says that the whole men's movement is about dancing with grief. I felt an echo of that sentiment in the dance you were describing in your song.

RANDALL: The question is, whose grief is it? His or the audience's?

STEWART: What about Beach Boys? Do you do any Beach Boys?

ROBIN: It's the dual grief of the bee and the flower. And Andy's right. Grief is the cornerstone of the men's movement.

RANDALL: You mean self-indulgence is the cornerstone of the men's movement.

STEWART: OK. Maybe a tune wasn't the right idea. Why don't we try some of that breathing thing, that in-out thing, you know, center-of-the-earth, top-of-the-head stuff?

ROBIN: I'd suggest we try a naming ceremony but we don't have a crystal.

STEWART: We don't need to have the crystal, do we? *(hands ROBIN a rock lying on the ground)* How about if we use this, Robb?

ROBIN: Please don't call me Robb anymore! My name is Robin and we can't just use any old rock. It has to be a conductor, a spiritual vessel . . .

STEWART: *(takes a final swig of beer and hands ROBIN the empty bottle)* Well, how about this? It's kinda like crystal.

ROBIN: You want to imbue a beer bottle with psychic energy?

RANDALL: Aw come on, Robb. It's just a symbol after all. It gets its power from what you put into it.

STEWART: It's sorta the same color as your crystal. *(Holds it up.)* Sometimes you can see things in it.

ROBIN: Oh good, we're going to have a psychedelic experience with a beer bottle.

STEWART: One time I got a bottle with a dead mouse in it. It's true. I took it back to the ALCB and they gave me a whole case, for free.

RANDALL: *(at the same time as STEWART, nods)* For free.

ANDY: Well, what do you think, Robin? Do you want to try a naming ceremony with the beer bottle as a substitute crystal?

STEWART: *(hands ROBIN the beer bottle)* Yeah, gwan, take a whack at it.

ROBIN: I dunno, Andy. I feel there's a sort of psychic vacuum around this campfire.

ANDY: You have to remember that you've had a great deal more experience in this area than Randall or Stewart. You'd expect a little skepticism, wouldn't you?

ROBIN: I suppose.

RANDALL: Sure. You're an expert in all this, we're the stupid Philistines. So tell us, what's a naming ceremony?

ROBIN: A naming ceremony is designed to discover a man's true name. The name he carries deep in his soul, the one that best expresses his inner self.

RANDALL: What's yours? Rhumbas with Rabbits?

ROBIN: *(leaps up, furious)* Oh, that's it! That's enough. We'll just forget about having a meaningful men's weekend. Let's just sit out here and stick with our blind, male behavior patterns.

STEWART: Ah, Robin. Don't be upset. Come on, what was your name?

ROBIN: I'm not telling.

ANDY: Why don't you tell them, Robin. They won't laugh.

ROBIN: Yes, they will.

RANDALL: No, we promise. Boy Scout's honor.

ROBIN: I don't believe you.

STEWART: No, really. Tell us.

ROBIN: No! My other name is very special and I'm not going to just lay it out for you guys to ridicule. Absolutely not! I will not tell you!

A long pause.

STEWART: Well, I could play a song—

Grabs the empty bottle and holds it up.

ROBIN: Ra Ho Tep.

They ALL roar with laughter. ANDY struggles to contain his amusement.

ROBIN: See, I knew it.

RANDALL: Ra Ho Tep?

ANDY: Now we promised.

ROBIN: I discovered about two years ago at a Past Life Regression workshop that I used to be an Egyptian holy man in about 430 B.C.

RANDALL: Oh my God, we've got a sick puppy here.

ROBIN points to the bottle.

ROBIN: I believe I have the floor.

RANDALL: Sorry.

ROBIN: I'm telling you, this is the real thing. The workshop was led by Jay Zee Knight *(dramatic pause. Waits for reaction but doesn't get it}* You know, the medium who channeled for Shirley MacLaine?

STEWART
& RANDALL: Ohhhhh . . .

ROBIN: I was keeper of the sacred temple of Osiris near Luxor *(pause. Leans forward, dramatic)* But I was murdered . . .

RANDALL: I can believe that.

ROBIN: For political reasons. I won't get into the details because you wouldn't understand but suffice it to say that my quest for spiritual enlightenment goes back many lifetimes. I am what they call "a seeker". And a seeker is always mocked and misunderstood. Especially by those whose only goal in life is to sleep with an entire sorority.

RANDALL: Are you finished?

ROBIN: Yes.

RANDALL reaches over, takes the beer bottle from ROBIN and holds it up to show that he has the floor.

RANDALL: OK. I've been listening to you all day go on and on about how enlightened you are and how you've got all the answers for the modern man. Well, if you've got it figured out, how come you feel the need to go to every New Age mumbo-jumbo workshop that comes along? I mean, get a life, Robin. Your own life.

ROBIN: That just shows how much you know about—

RANDALL: *(holds up the beer bottle)* Uh uh . . . my turn. You started out talking about some flaky naming ceremony and a fifteen-foot wooden penis and then suddenly you're talking past life regression and Shirley MacLaine's channeler for God's sake! This stuff is all interchangeable to you, isn't it?

STEWART: *(takes the last swallow from his beer bottle and holds it up)* You want to know what I think?

ROBIN &
RANDALL: No!

ROBIN: It's a cumulative process, Randall—

RANDALL: *(waves the beer bottle at him)* Uh uh . . . I think you're so desperately bored with yourself that you'd buy into any half-witted, self-help con game that's going. Let's just do a little survey here. You can answer by nodding your head for yes or shaking it for no. Have you ever had dinner with the Hare Krishna?

ROBIN hesitates, then nods.

RANDALL: Have you ever taken a scientology personality test?

ROBIN nods again.

RANDALL: Are your best friends therapists?

ROBIN nods again, with a hang-dog look. RANDALL continues.

RANDALL: Have you ever been Rolfed? Did you participate in the cosmic convergence? Have you ever had a colonic? Do you own a Ravi Shankar record?

ROBIN lunges at RANDALL and tries to grab the beer bottle away as RANDALL continues, holding the bottle just out of range.

RANDALL: Have you ever been on an est weekend? Do you own a tape with only the sounds of falling rain on it? Are you now or have you ever been an Amway distributor?

ROBIN grabs another beer bottle and holds it up.

ROBIN: There have to be seekers willing to take chances! Yes, and willing to make mistakes, if necessary. For the sake of the planet!

RANDALL: Don't forget the baby seals.

ROBIN: *(spouting, sputtering)* We have to re-invent what it means to be a man! And we have to do it quickly, before the planet is destroyed!

RANDALL: You don't give a shit about the planet. You're so self absorbed there's no room in your psyche for anyone but you. All of you. Ra Ho Tep, Shirley MacLaine, Bunny Stalker . . . When was the last time you had something in your life that wasn't about you, that wasn't about breathing through your anus or analyzing your poor long-suffering father . . .

ROBIN: Leave my father out of it.

RANDALL: All that shit about mythopoetic heritage! Your father probably can't stand to be around you. Just like everyone else.

ROBIN stops. RANDALL realizes he's gone too far. Then ROBIN bursts into tears.

ROBIN: *(through the sobs)* My father died when I was ten years old. *(continues to sob relentlessly)*

The other men are initially paralyzed by his weeping and don't know what to do.

STEWART: *(embarrassed by the crying)* Aww, Jesus, Robb . . .

ANDY: That's OK, Robin, let it go . . .

RANDALL: Wait a second! This isn't fair! This is how women get out of arguments!

ROBIN: *(continues sobbing)* I can't help it!

RANDALL: It's Pavlovian. Men go into a coma at the sight of tears.

ROBIN: You're supposed to cry over your father on weekends like this! I loved my dad.

RANDALL takes a deep breath and goes over to ROBIN. He sits beside him as ROBIN continues to sob. After a pause, he puts his arm around ROBIN's shoulder.

RANDALL: (*sympathetic*) It's OK. You should be able to cry if you want.

ROBIN: It's not like I try to be an asshole, you know? I know I'm self-absorbed. Don't you think I know that? I'm thirty-eight and I've lived alone all my adult life. I watched my mother grow old alone. I'm scared it'll happen to me.

RANDALL: I know how you feel.

ROBIN: Oh, sure. How would you know?

RANDALL: My dad died when I was fifteen.

ROBIN and RANDALL look at each other: a moment of recognition. STEWART goes over to the guitar and picks it up. He starts to strum Neil Young's "Heart of Gold."

STEWART: (*straining, it's way too high for him*) I wanna live . . . I wanna give . . . I've been a miner for a heart of gold . . .

STEWART
& RANDALL: It's these expressions . . . I never give . . .

ALL: That keep me searchin' for a heart of gold . . . and I'm gettin' old . . . keep me searchin' for a heart of gold and I'm getting old . . .

Stage lights go down and the music is cross-faded into Neil Young's version of the song.

Scene Six

Music: We hear the next verse of "Heart of Gold" and then the music fades down during the harmonica instrumental. Stage lights rise on the four sleeping wild guys. They are all tucked into their sleeping bags around the smoldering fire. It is dead of night now and the stars twinkle overhead. Suddenly there is a rustling sound offstage.

STEWART: *(sits up)* What was that?

The others sit up groggily.

RANDALL: Huh?

STEWART: I heard something in the bushes.

ANDY: Is something out there?

STEWART: Shhhh. Listen.

ROBIN: *(getting up excited)* It's a rabbit! I caught a rabbit in the snare! All right! *(he hesitates)*

RANDALL: Well, you better go and get it.

ROBIN: I could go and get it in the morning.

RANDALL: It might be suffering.

STEWART: Yeah, you better go and . . . you know . . . finish it off.

ROBIN: *(to STEWART)* Do you wanna go? You're sort of a northern guy.

STEWART: Sorry. I work in produce.

ANDY: You better go and check it out, Robin.

RANDALL: I hate to think of that poor little bunny, garroted in the moonlight. Thrashing his little cottontail back and forth . . . Remember in the Godfather when Luka Brazzi—

ROBIN: OK. OK, I'm going!

ROBIN reluctantly goes offstage.

STEWART: We're not gonna put bunny blood on our faces, are we?

ANDY: No.

RANDALL: Where did you meet Robin, anyway? He's sort of an unlikely pal for you.

ANDY: He showed up at our men's group one night. I think he was just lonely. I know he's a little hard to take at times, but I like him. I like his sincerity.

ROBIN: *(offstage)* Oh my God!!

ROBIN comes back on the fly.

ROBIN: That's no bunny out there!

RANDALL: You're no bunny till some bunny loves you.

ROBIN: IT'S A BEAR!!!

They all leap up in a panic.

ROBIN: *(searching in a panic)* Where's my spear? Where's my spear?

STEWART: I really hate bears . . . I really hate bears . . . I really hate bears—

ANDY: Now, just calm down.

RANDALL: No one said anything about us *being* breakfast.

ANDY: It's OK. It's most likely just a common black bear. They're nocturnal feeders . . . he's probably looking for berries or an ant hill . . .

RANDALL: Or a late-night lawyer snack.

ANDY: *(putting sticks on the fire)* We'll build the fire up and he'll move on . . . no trouble . . .

Sound offstage: the rustling in the bushes is coming closer. STEWART looks over at RANDALL. There's a pause.

RANDALL: What about you, Robin? Are you scared of bears?

ROBIN: You're damn right I'm scared of bears. Are you kidding? Do you realize that—

RANDALL whacks ROBIN in the knee with his stick, then keeps tapping.

ROBIN: Ow! *(looks at RANDALL, then smiles, starts to tap his stick)* No, I'm not scared a bears. I hate 'em.

ROBIN, STEWART and RANDALL grin at each other and start tapping their sticks louder.

RANDALL: Yeah. We aren't scared a bears. But we sure hate 'em!

STEWART: *(grinning)* Yeah!

RANDALL,
ROBIN &
STEWART: *(a chant)* We aren't scared a bears! But we sure hate 'em!

RANDALL: What about you, Andy? You hate bears too, right?

ANDY: No. I really like bears. And I'm not afraid of them, either. I respect them, but I'm not afraid of them.

They ALL stop tapping their sticks.

RANDALL: Jesus.

ANDY: But I liked what you were doing just now. Acknowledging the fear you have in common by denying it in a ritualistic way. Keep going if you want.

ROBIN: Somehow we've lost the spontaneity of the moment.

ANDY: Men are taught to suppress fear. It's equated with courage in our culture but nothing could be farther from the truth. For modern men, the expression of their deepest inner fears may be the single most courageous act of their lives.

RANDALL: So you're not scared of bears. But you're scared of something, right?

ANDY: Everyone's afraid of something.

RANDALL: So? What is it for you?

ANDY doesn't answer.

ROBIN: Well, I'm afraid of women.

RANDALL: Did your analyst tell you that?

ROBIN: Well, yeah. But it's true. I don't know how to behave with them.

RANDALL: It's just a matter of self-confidence. Women want you to act like you know what you're doing. Even if you don't.

ROBIN: I get so confused. I can't seem to keep a relationship going. The last time, it was this woman, Lorraine. She's a regular customer down at the Eco-Shop, where I work part-time. Anyway, every time she came in we'd have these great conversations over the crushed-glass bin. But it still took me a year and a half to work up the courage to ask her out. We go to this cappuccino bar and I'm so nervous, I knock back three double lattes and I'm like, hovering six inches above the stool. After awhile, she gets this glazed look in her eyes. Hasn't returned one of my calls since. I don't know. Maybe I try too hard.

STEWART: This one time, when I was just out of high school, I got a date with that year's Miss Lone Pine. It was a big deal, you know—I borrowed a friend's pick-up and everything *(bats his own head)* I went to kiss her and wound up elbowing her in the nose. She starts bleeding all over the cab so I go to hand her some Kleenex, right, and my ID bracelet rips her dress. She freaks out, like she thinks I'm attacking her. I wasn't! I mean, I'm not that kind of guy!

RANDALL: No one ever explains this stuff when you're a teenager. You're just supposed to *know* how to behave with girls.

ROBIN: Yeah, like someone goes presto . . . you're Prince Charles.

RANDALL: Prince Charles?

STEWART: Anyway, that's the great thing about my wife, Maxie, eh? I don't have to put on a bunch of phony stuff for her. She loves me for what I am, you know? Even if I mess up sometimes.

ROBIN: Women are the most frustrating, indecipherable, completely unfathomable mystery in the world! All the women I've ever gone out with wanted me to be someone else.

RANDALL: *(teasing)* And you were.

ROBIN gives RANDALL a dirty look. Then they both smile.

STEWART: This is sorta cool, you know? I never talk about stuff like this with the guys on the ball team.

ROBIN: Well, maybe you should.

STEWART: *(laughs)* Are you outta your mind? *(thinks of an example)* This guy, Steve? I play ball with him twice a week, right? His wife left him two months ago. I find out the day before yesterday! Man!

ANDY: The break-up of a relationship can be one of the hardest things to talk about. And to understand.

STEWART: But like we're buddies, right? We see each other all the time. Why wouldn't he tell me?

ANDY: Dr. Rothenberg says that the natural impulse is to protect the wound from your own social circle. It's often falsely perceived as a personal failure, a betrayal of society's contract. There's a lot of guilt attached—

RANDALL: *(finally tired of all this)* Andy. We're talking about Stewart's friend here and you're still dishing out psychosocial theory.

ANDY: You need to be able to step back and learn as you go along. In the same way that Tai Chi teaches you to absorb your opponent's energy and rechannel it.

RANDALL: Well, that's great for Buddhist monks. But what about Steve? We're talking about a real person here.

ANDY: I was just trying to make the point that guilt is a very strong emotion.

ROBIN: No kidding. I feel guilty all the time. Especially with women. Starting with my mother. She made me feel guilty for everything. Even the fact that my father wasn't around anymore.

RANDALL: That wasn't your fault.

ROBIN: I know, but the guilt is still there. I feel guilty when I hear the newest violence against women statistics. I feel guilty about sexism on MTV. I feel guilty about inequality in the workplace . . .

RANDALL: The hole in the ozone . . .

ROBIN: Yeah, that one's my fault too. Laundry detergent commercials. The slave-trade of the seventeenth century, the industrial revolution . . .

RANDALL: Willie and Julio . . .

STEWART: I feel guilty about leaving the toilet seat up . . .

ROBIN: All the unresolved North American Native land claims, the automobile, PCBs . . .

STEWART: PMS.

RANDALL: Not getting pregnant.

ROBIN: The pill, breast implants, high-heeled shoes . . .

RANDALL: Paul Anka.

ROBIN: I feel like I've absorbed responsibility for every rotten thing that's ever happened on the planet just because I have a penis. So, I have all these wonderful empathetic talks with women about how men have screwed up the world and . . .

RANDALL: *(at the same time as ROBIN)* They all think you're a wimp.

ROBIN: They all think I'm a wimp. So I go out on a few men's retreats to try and discover what being a modern, responsible man is about and now they're calling me . . .

RANDALL: Anti-feminist.

ROBIN: Anti-feminist. I'm sorry but I read Doris Lessing novels, I go to the feminist film festivals. I would never personally pay a woman less than a man for the same job. I don't tell sexist jokes. I know there's a lot of bad asses out there but I'M NOT ONE OF THEM!!

ANDY: It doesn't have to be so confrontational. Barbara and I have found a balance that works for us.

RANDALL: Oh, Maharishi, please tell us what it is . . .

ANDY: She has an absorbing and fulfilling career. I have an absorbing and fulfilling career.

RANDALL: And you meet in Moose Jaw every six months.

ANDY: It's true we don't see each other as much as we'd like to but, it's part of being intellectually active and living a full life.

RANDALL: Intellectually active is kind of an understatement, don't you think?

ANDY: What do you mean?

RANDALL: The last twenty-four hours have been like you're the twelve-year-old and we're the ant farm. I mean, this group isn't totally equal, is it? We're not exactly the four musketeers. One for all and all for one.

ROBIN: Yeah, Randall's right. We're hangin' out all over the place here and you're making notes. I've known you for two years and I didn't know you had a wife. You've never talked about her.

ANDY: Well, I do have a wife. *(beat)* I have a teenage son as well.

RANDALL: *(surprised)* You have a son? So, you're the absent father that Bly talks about. How come you didn't bring your son?

ANDY: He couldn't come.

RANDALL: Why not? What about quality time? How come you brought us out here and left your own kid at home?

ANDY: I couldn't bring Danny.

STEWART: Why not?

ANDY: *(big pause)* He's on probation. He's not allowed out of the city.

The guys are all a little bit shocked. They pause.

STEWART: What did he do?

ANDY: *(with difficulty)* He vandalized a graveyard. A Jewish graveyard. I don't know why. A year in therapy later and I still don't know why. Where does that come from? Me? In some way I can't understand?

ROBIN: Well, you have your wife. You have each other to lean on.

STEWART: My brother stole a car when he was sixteen and got busted, but he turned out to be a good guy. Who knows why young guys do some of the things they do, eh? Mom and Dad stuck with him and he was OK, you know?

RANDALL: The important thing is there're two of you.

ANDY throws his spear on the fire, walks to the far edge of the stage and turns his back to the others.

ANDY: Did you know that in many primitive tribes, boys are kidnapped by the men of the village at a certain age to symbolize their passage from the world of women to the world of men? Often a physical wound is inflicted to be a constant reminder that the boy is now initiated.

ROBIN: Andy. Come and sit by the fire with us.

ANDY: *(back still to the group)* There are so many literary references. The idea of male initiation is embedded in the collective unconscious . . .

RANDALL: Andy? Don't bullshit us, OK? If you don't want to talk to us, that's all right. But don't bullshit us.

ROBIN: A guy doesn't go out and turn over all these psychological stones for the hell of it. A person searches because they're missing something. Come back to the fire.

ANDY pauses, then comes back to the fire and sits down.

RANDALL: It's not a sin to talk about yourself, Andy.

STEWART: Look, you set up this whole weekend so we could get in touch with our feelings. But, like, you're the only one not doin' it. How come?

ANDY: I don't think I know how.

RANDALL: (gently) Yes, you do.

The other guys wait.

ANDY: *(takes a deep breath)* The thing with Danny, it's ruined our marriage. Or our marriage ruined Danny. I don't know which. *(pause)* Barbara's having an affair. She doesn't know that I know. But I do. I don't blame her, really. I understand that she needed someone, I just . . .

STEWART shakes his head and puts a hand on ANDY's shoulder.

STEWART: Oh, man.

ANDY: *(struggling)* There's something . . . (hand to his chest) . . . in here. I don't know what, something brooding, dangerous . . . I feel like everything I've done, all these years . . . that it's all been for nothing . . . or worse, much worse . . .

RANDALL: You're pissed off, Andy. Admit it.

ANDY: *(stands up again and begins to pace, angrily)* All right. Yes!
                  I am pissed off! I am . . . *(trembling)* outraged! My son is
                  embracing everything I despise in this world . . . I have this
                  . . . urge, this overwhelming urge to break his rotten neck!
                  And my wife . . . she's abandoned us both, exactly when
                  we needed her most! How could she do such a thing!!?

*ANDY grips his spear so fiercely that he may lash out at anything.
Suddenly, the rage seems to pass.*

ROBIN: Let your anger go.

ANDY: *(shaking his head)* No.

ROBIN: Come on, Andy. Let it out! You're mad as hell, you need to
                  let it out!

ANDY: No. *(gives the spear back to ROBIN)*

ROBIN: But, you need to physicalize your rage . . .

ANDY: No, Robin, I don't. *(more quietly)* I don't need to vent
                  my anger on a bush, or paint my face, or anything else.
                  What I need is time to think. I need to . . . start again
                  somehow. *(shakes his head)* I'm fifty years old and I still
                  don't understand anything. *(beat)* I feel so . . . lost.

RANDALL: *(puts his hand on ANDY's other shoulder, says kindly)*
                  Well, guess what, brother? We're all hopelessly fucking
                  lost. And we always have been. *(big pause)* But there is
                  one great satisfaction in all this.

ROBIN: *(breathlessly)* What?

RANDALL: At least we know . . . *(points at STEWART)* IT'S ALL HIS
                  FAULT!!!

*STEWART is taken aback at first. But RANDALL starts to smile. ANDY
and ROBIN start to laugh. Soon they're all laughing.*

Sound offstage: the loud rustling in the bushes.

ROBIN: Oh, my God! He's back.

They all leap up and grab their spears. ANDY picks up the drum.

STEWART: Go away!

RANDALL: G'wan. Get outta here, you stupid bear!

ANDY: *(beating the drum in time)* Go bruin go!

They all stop and look at ANDY, a little surprised, then . . .

ALL: Go bruin go! Go bruin go! Go bruin go!!!

They all start leaping around the fire to the beat of the drum, screaming at the top of their lungs and laughing foolishly at each other. "Go bruins go!" becomes a hockey-arena chant.

ALL: Go bruins go! Go bruins go! Go bruins go!

Stage lights go down.

Scene Seven

Stage lights come up as the music fades down. It's morning. The wild guys, minus ANDY, are lying in their sleeping bags. STEWART wakes up first.

STEWART: *(looking around)* Hey, where's Andy?

RANDALL: Probably communing with nature somewhere.

ROBIN: Hey, Andy's pack is gone.

STEWART: What?

RANDALL: He couldn't have gone far. It's not like he knows the way home.

ROBIN: I dunno. It was kind of a breakthrough for him last night. Maybe he just, you know, couldn't face us this morning.

STEWART: Maybe he tried to go back alone.

RANDALL: Andy wouldn't leave us behind . . . we're the four musketeers, right?

ROBIN: I thought we were the four stooges.

RANDALL: *(smiles)* Yeah, well, that was yesterday.

ANDY walks on stage, pack on his back. He's carrying a large A&W bag.

ANDY: Morning, guys.

STEWART: Where were you?

ANDY sits by the fire pit, opens the bag. He starts pulling out Bacon N' Eggers, hash browns, etc. The others look at him, paralyzed.

ANDY: It's a beautiful day, isn't it? Listen, I hope everyone likes *(reads the packaging)* Bacon N' Eggers. I figured you guys might be a little hungry so I got lots of these hash brown things.

RANDALL: It's a mirage, Stewart. It'll pass.

ANDY: *(opens a Bacon N' Egger and waves it in front of the guys)* Mmmm. It's real.

The wild guys fall on the A&W bag like a pack of ravenous wolves.

ANDY: Turns out we camped a mile from the highway. It's interesting, isn't it? Being lost isn't a physical condition, it's a mental condition. If we had known yesterday, for example . . .

RANDALL: Andy? Shut up and give us the ketchup.

ANDY playfully squirts ketchup at RANDALL. RANDALL grabs a ketchup packet and squirts some back. STEWART and ROBIN join in. They all get into the act, smearing ketchup on their faces and dancing around the fire pit, a group of friends at last.

End of play.

Shopaholic

By Glenda Stirling

Shopaholic was commissioned by the Petro-Canada Stage One Plays. It premiered October 7, 2002 at Lunchbox Theatre, Calgary, with the following cast.

ABIGAIL ADAMS:	Esther Purves-Smith
WOMEN:	Karen Johnson-Diamond
MEN:	Ryan Luhning

Directed by Johanne Deleeuw

Set and Lighting Design by Colin Ross

Costumes by Brian Craik

Stage Manager: Michael Howard

Production Manager: Laura Lee Billing

Technical Director: William Bourque

Shopaholic was originally workshopped as part of the Petro-Canada Stage One Plays in May of 2002 with Esther Purves-Smith (Abigail Adams), Suzanne McDowel (Women) and Trevor Leigh (Men). The workshop was directed by Gail Hanrahan. The Stage Manager was Michael Howard. Stage directions were read by Brianna Moench.

Characters
ABIGAIL ADAMS
WOMEN (played by one actor): LINDA
                                         CASH GIRL
                                         SALES GIRL
                                         JOY
                                         GRANDMA
                                         INTERCOM
                                         MOM
                                         VOICE
MEN (played by one actor): MR. BANKS
                                         TOUGH GUY
                                         BOYFRIEND #3
                                         THE ONE

ABIGAIL stands in the middle of the stage. Bland, regular old meeting hall lighting. A Shopaholics self-help meeting. The house lights are in.

ABBY: Hello . . . Hi there! Jeez. Glad you could come. Ahhh. . . . I can't really tell how many of you are out there. . . . Well, I can see there is a lot. Um, but if a lot is like, forty or two hundred, I can't really tell. Well. I could count, I suppose. 1, 2, 3, 4, 5, 6, 7, 8, 9, 10, 11, 12, 13 . . . Well, it doesn't really matter. Which is not to say you don't matter. You really do matter. A lot. And I am just really glad that we could all meet here and . . . Heal together. God, that sounds dorky. Um . . . . So.

              Well, to start, I noticed that some of you out there have a bag. A shopping bag, not handbags or gym bags. But you there, Miss, that little purse is truly great. . . . but that is not the point. The point is I know some of you out there have bags. Bags from stores. Bags from stores with articles purchased from those stores inside. Raise you hands if that's you. Go on. Don't be afraid. You won't be punished here. Good. Now if the bag has only food in it, drop your hand. If it has only toilet paper, shaving cream, condoms, and other life-saving personal-care items, drop your hand. If you have facial scrubs, mascara, perfume, or blotting paper in there you need to keep your hand up. They just don't qualify as life-saving personal items. I know, it is hard to believe. I didn't believe it either, but that is why we are all here . . . Good. Now, anyone with baby-care items, like talc and Q-tips and diapers and stuff, you may also drop your hand. However, if you have cute baby clothes or toys, and you do not actually have children of your own, you must keep your hand up. Those things are part of your disease.

Anywho, those of you with your hands up, pat yourself on the back. That's right, pat yourself on the back because this could be the last time you ever impulse-buy something you don't need. Honestly it could be. I believe it. Ladies, and you sir, this could be the last day of your life as a junkie. An addict. Oh, you will Jones all right, and it will suck, and your hands will shake as they reach out to touch the good stuff, as you consider selling your car to finance the latest spree . . . It will suck.

But now my friends, we have each other. And I will start us off. You should know, that I've never started anything in my life, other than diets. Certainly nothing on this scale. But I believe one generally starts with the story of Rock Bottom. I don't have a rock bottom, I have a Black Friday, which ended up as Good Friday. The first Friday of the rest of my life.

Blackout.

Lights up. ABBY sits across a desk from the MR. BANKS, the bank manager.

ABBY: Thank you for meeting me, Mr. Banks. Sorry my time was so inflexible, but the marketing field is very busy. Between the hours of 1 and 2 p.m. is the only time I can afford not to have an idea about marketing.

MR. BANKS: Yes.

ABBY: That, by the way, is a very nice tie. Not too bold, but rich enough not to be boring. I just love autumn colors, they are so great. . . .

               So. To get down to it. My mortgage application.

Pause.

ABBY: So. I've been approved, right?

MR. BANKS: Yes.

ABBY: This is just fantastic.

Pause.

ABBY: Right, so how much is it?

MR. BANKS slides a piece of paper across to her. ABBY looks at it.

ABBY: There seems to be some kind of a . . . mistake here.

Pause.

ABBY: It seems I have been approved for a $60,000 mortgage. And that is great. Except for I live in this city, right? Where a one-bedroom-five-hundred-square-foot-north-facing-basement-condo is looking to sell at about $120,000. Now, I don't want to live in a five-hundred-square-foot-north-facing-basement-condo. So, so far, so good. The little problem is I would like to live in a slightly better place, and according to this . . . assessment, I could only afford half of a crap condo. So, maybe like, 250 square feet under a bridge somewhere, waiting for the Billy Goat Gruff. . . .

Pause.

ABBY: You ever read that?

MR. BANKS: No.

ABBY: So, I am thinking this is some kind of a typo, and you left a one off the front, or a zero off the back, or something like that. Why don't you just take a look at it and see what we can do?

ABBY leans over the desk, holding out the paper file. Meanwhile the MR. BANKS hits a button on his computer. She looks at his screen. It's like an FBI file of her life.

ABBY: Oh. Geez. Look at that. *(scrambling to put the papers away)* You can just pop my whole life up on your screen with your button. Wow. I'd just be checking up on people all the time. Wow . . . Ummm, so, do you see the mistake, the typo, the thing?

Pause.

ABBY: I mean, I don't make, what like, a bank manager makes, but, I mean, I do have to pay taxes so I must make something OK.

MR. BANKS: You appear to have an income.

ABBY: Right. So, if you could just explain to me how someone with a good job, a good job with a good, reputable firm, a business firm, in a professional field, could only get approval for $60,000, which would not buy squat . . . but instead force me to squat, that would be fantastic.

Three giant credit cards fly in from the ceiling. They are Amex, MC and Visa.

ABBY: I see. Actually, I don't.

I mean, I got those things in the first place, oh years ago, to get myself a credit rating, so I could get a car loan . . . Which I did. Unfortunately Boyfriend # 3 took the car when we broke up and he drove back to Inuvik, may the sun never rise on his face again, but the point is . . . Those cards help me. Without them you wouldn't even look at a mortgage application. So what exactly is the problem?

MR. BANKS: Balance.

ABBY: I have balance. I work out on balance balls, I go to aromatherapy therapy and singles soccer to ensure I have balance. I have a balanced life.

Pause.

ABBY: I see. But, everyone has credit card debt? Now, don't they? I mean we all do. That is why there are banks, Mr. Banks. And, I have always paid the minimum on my cards, before or on the due date? Right?

MR. BANKS: Yes.

ABBY: So that is an excellent thing for the credit rating, isn't it? The paying the minimum every month on time leads to excellent credit ratings, does it not? So the problem would be?

A giant budget flies down from the ceiling. Clearly about half of what the total budget is goes to pay minimum credit card payments.

ABBY: Right. So, if I have been paying that enormous amount faithfully for this many years, then clearly I could continue to pay it, as I pay it now. The only difference would be, of course, that I would also be paying a mortgage. Investing In My Future, as they say on your commercials.

Pause.

ABBY: Or do you think that impossible?

MR. BANKS: Yes.

ABBY: Right. Well, that leaves us at a bit of a loss. As far as Investing In My Future, which I would really like to do, and as your commercials keep telling me I should do. I have three credit cards with this bank. And I've paid them, and . . . My god, are you telling me I should cut up my credit cards?

MR. BANKS: No! no-no-no-no! *(the first time we hear any emotion in his voice)*

ABBY: Good. Because I would really hate to do that. They're good for emergencies and stuff.

MR. BANKS: Yes.

ABBY: And I pay the minimum, and the interest, every month—

MR. BANKS: Yes.

ABBY: And sometimes I even put a big lump down on them—

MR. BANKS: Yes, yes. No cutting. Keep the cards.

ABBY: Well, thank God for that, eh? That's just great! Thank you for that. I am so glad that we both agree I really need those cards.

MR. BANKS: You really need the cards.

ABBY: Alrighty then! Now about the mortgage. So I guess the thing is, I need to earn more, or spend less, or something like that, right? I read that in The Rich Hairdresser. Right, so if I just had more money to spend on mortgage payments, then you would give me a bigger mortgage, even though what I pay now for rent is higher than a mortgage. I get it. I really do, I am really quite good with numbers. Make more, spend less, and you'll give me a bigger mortgage, right?

MR. BANKS: Possibly.

ABBY: Well, that is great, a clear course of action, some goals, we are all pulling together in the same boat and heading in the same direction. Fabulous. I am gonna get out of here, and grab some lunch, and thanks again for that. Really, it was just fantastic.

Lights shift. Back to the Shopaholics meeting.

ABBY: I was standing with my back against the wall, the wall of the bank, in the mall. And all these people were walking by me, happy people. People with mortgages, and houses and cars and bags. And I felt like I was really not one of them. I felt like I was from another planet. Another planet far, far away, and the mother ship was never coming back.

I couldn't help thinking—Why am I so different from them? Why do they get to have a house and a job and a mortgage and a Mate and matching furniture? I was positively Dickensian in my dejection. I was Little Dorrit. I was Oliver. I am holding out my bowl to the universe and saying – "Please Sir, can I have some more?"

And then I saw her—Linda, the receptionist, who has my old job. The job I had until two years ago, when I got a raise and a bigger title, Administrative Assistant to the Gen X Accounts Marketing Rep. And I happen to know she has a mortgage. And a husband, and a mouthful of straight white teeth. All things I hated in that moment. And she was coming closer and closer and closer, until her big featured face was right up close to mine.

Lights shift to the mall.

LINDA: Abby! How nice to see you. How are you?

ABBY: *(to the audience)* How am I? How nice to see me? Like she didn't just see me forty-five minutes ago?

LINDA: What are you doing here? Oh, of course, your meeting with the bank. How did that go?

ABBY: Great. Just great. I got a mortgage. I just need to iron out a few kinks.

LINDA: Great. You must be really pleased with yourself. That must feel really good. You know, moving forward?

ABBY: Forward?

LINDA: You know, moving into the future, a new stage of life, adulthood.

ABBY: Right. Of course I know. Is that what this is? Adulthood?

LINDA: Well, buying a house . . .

ABBY: Buying adulthood . . .

LINDA: Always striving, moving ahead, reaching for the next thing.

ABBY: Right, reaching.

LINDA: And I always knew you were like that Abby, no matter what anyone said, I knew you were—

ABBY: —What?

LINDA: What, what?

ABBY: What do people say? Say about me? Me not reaching?

LINDA: No—I didn't mean—nothing. Nothing. No one says anything . . . specific.

ABBY: How about in general, Linda?

LINDA: Generally I always knew you'd want to move up. In the world. Ahead. And I do too. We are alike in that forward momentum motion. Going forward. Like your old job. You moved on. And I moved in. And that will happen again. Forward motion.

ABBY: You're moving in on my job?

LINDA: Of course not! Not your job, of course. Just looking forward to moving forward, which of course you are also doing, or there would be a traffic jam.

ABBY: Traffic jam?

LINDA: Well, way to go, you go-getter you! Way to move forward! You must feel great.

ABBY: Actually, I don't feel so good. Actually, when I was in the bank manager's office I got this awful cramping in my stomach. Yup. Serious diarrhea. Like I am going to explode from every orifice.

I don't think I'll be in for the rest of the day. In fact, I think I better find a toilet before my butt blows off.

Lights Shift. Back in the Shopaholics meeting.

ABBY: Abigail Adams. That's me. With initials like A.A, I always kind of knew that I was destined for some serious addictions. I could see it coming a mile away. I started reading up on it early.

I've always kind of hoped it could be gambling, REAL gambling, not scratch and wins. At least that way my addiction would be kind of glamorous, possibly involve winning some money, and definitely involve dating high-rollers. Didn't happen. Any kind of gambling makes me very anxious. Throwing money away like that, fiscal irresponsibility, gives me hives. Ironic, I know.

Then I thought, maybe heroin. I mean, if you must become addicted to something, heroin is definitely the over achiever of the addictions. And, to top it all off, while costing a fortune and probably killing you over an alarmingly short period of time, it will ensure waif like thinness.

Come on folks. Look at me. A little waif-like thinness would go down really well in my life.

But no. I never did develop an addiction to any of the glamour stuff. In fact, as far as I could tell, I made it alarmingly free from addictions. Ok, so I drink sometimes, did some pot in high school and probably smoke too many cigarettes, but on the whole, unremarkable. No addiction in sight. Just a humdrum job in a marketing firm and a dependence on retail therapy.

Lights shift. Drug Store Music.

Over the store intercom:

INTERCOM: Good afternoon shoppers. Today we are pleased to offer you the Buyers Drug Mart Platinum Card. The more you buy, the more you save, some restrictions apply. Buyers Drug Mart Platinum Card holders will receive special discounts, randomly and periodically, dependent on our whims and overstocking. Enjoy your shopping, and ask at the sales counter about the new Buyers Drug Mart Platinum Cards.

ABBY is walking up and down the aisles of the drug store. Her basket is full.

ABBY: Bubble bath. No-name. Musk. Because anything fruity or floral or citrus makes me smell like cat pee. My grandmother assured me of this when I was nine.

GRANDMA   Abby. You stink. What the heck do you have on yourself? Perfume, eh? Some Avon flowery crap, no doubt. Don't bother. You are not a delicate flower, my girl. You are solid, strong like bull. On a husky woman that stuff smells wrong. People smell that and they think they see what is coming, some small red-headed thing with blue eyes. And then what do they get? You. That is disappointing. Don't disappoint folks, Abby. Pick something that smells like you. Besides, you're a sweater. And flowers and sweat smell like cat piss when you mix them up.

ABBY: So. Musk, which I think goes well with sweat. And I'm pretty sure that musk is sexy, and if I wear it, I am too. Two bottles, because sometimes they run out. Moisturizing lotion, Landers—$1.98, with cocoa butter. Oh, and the no-name pimple prevention face cream, non-oily. Men's Triple Assault razor blade refills. Because I have yet to see a man's face that deserves more attention than my bikini line. Stumbled across that one when Boyfriend # 3, the same one who returned to the North that spawned him, caught me using his razor.

BOYFRIEND #3:   For Christ's sake, Abs, you don't use a man's razor on your legs! You are making me butcher my face! For Christ's sake! Look at me! I'm a mess.

ABBY: He was right. He was a mess. And it had nothing, or at least very little, to do with the toilet paper stuck all over his face. He left me, taking my car and gas card with him, promising to pay me back when he was safely in Inuvik. Of course he never did, and in the long run it was a small price to pay for the discovery of the smoothest legs ever.

Some hair conditioner, the expensive kind, because you should never scrimp on hydration. Bottle of water for the same reason . . .

Though I have problems with the water. I know how much I'm supposed to drink, like ten of these a day, and I know water is good for living. And that—how hard is it? I mean, you just drink some water, right? And I think if I carry the water bottle, I will drink it more often. Thereby re-hydrating from the inside out, which may save me on moisturizers and conditioners in the long run, and help me detoxify and have dewy skin and regular bowel movements. So I think I should probably buy two, if it's gonna do all that.

Hair holder, nail polish, polish remover and file, a new lipstick because—

GRANDMA: Abby, you'll never be a pretty girl, too much like your mom, and you're just not built for pretty. But you could do handsome, once you grow into yourself. The key, my girl, is lippy. Don't bother with all that other crap. A glass of wine, a ciggy and a little lippy is all a woman needs to look attractive from the other side of the pub.

ABBY: So a little lippy, good old Cherries in the Snow. Because though Gran was wrong about a lot of things, she was right about the lippy. Good skin and some lippy can go a long way.

Sounds of the cash register going, and the CASH GIRL chatting on the phone.

CASH GIRL: So I said to him, like, that is so not going to happen, and he says to me, you know that it is, hold on a sec, the conditioner is two for the same price, do you want another one? Yeah?

ABBY: Yes.

CASH GIRL: Grab it on the way out. So anyway, then he starts like, totally freaking out, saying like, you saw the schedule posted and you are so working here on Friday, and so, now I am here and stuck in hell being nice to weirdos in the mall on Friday night instead of at the 'N Sync concert. Is that everything?

ABBY nods.

CASH GIRL: Yeah, it totally sucks. That's seventy-five-eighty-nine. So, I am here, but I am so not gonna be happy about it. There's your change, hold on a sec, have a great day. God, it's hell.

ABBY is walking out.

ABBY: Seventy-five-eighty-nine? Holy! That is like, the cost of . . . of something big, Like three toasters. A bed in a bag, winter boots. Not some bubble bath and conditioner. Right, my conditioner . . . .

ABBY crosses over, grabs her conditioner, and goes to exit the store. Much madness ensues, as alarms go off, she drops her bags, her arm is pinned behind her back by a large security TOUGH GUY.

TOUGH GUY: Hold it right there lady.

ABBY: What exactly can I do for you?

T. GUY: Empty your bags.

ABBY: Oh! I paid for the conditioner. This is a dumb mix up, you know. Here. Just look at this receipt. See?

T. GUY: We'll see about that. Empty your bags.

ABBY: Are you for serious?

TOUGH GUY continues to look at her.

ABBY: Fine.

ABBY dumps her shopping bag on the floor. ABBY watches TOUGH GUY down on his hands and knees, looking at the contents of the bag, and the receipt.

T. GUY: HA! You already had a bottle of conditioner in this bag. And you only paid for one, and you have two . . . Clearly theft!

ABBY: The conditioner was Two-For-One.

T. GUY: Not.

ABBY: Pardon?

T. GUY: Not.

ABBY: Was too.

T. GUY: Not.

ABBY: Too.

T. GUY: Empty your purse.

ABBY: Not.

Pause. ABBY dumps out her purse.

ABBY: There you have it. Pleased now? My wallet.

ABBY puts the wallet in her pocket.

T. GUY: *(as he examines the contents)* Two tampons. One, two, five lipsticks, one lip gloss. Geez. Eight hair clips. One tube of hand lotion, empty. Two empty packages of cigarettes, one full pack, three lighters, one notebook, three pens and a mediaeval mystery novel. Phone bill, LRT receipts, Tylenol cold tablets and a condom.

ABBY: Do you want to unwrap the condom or anything or make sure I'm not smuggling cocaine in sex things? Go ahead, I doubt I'll need it.

T. GUY: Empty your wallet.

ABBY: We've had a nice time, playing empty your bags, while we both know I haven't stolen anything. But I know you have a sad-sack pathetic life with very little joy, so with great pity I have gone along with your ridiculous demands . . .

          No. How do I know you are not going to copy down my credit card numbers and memorize my social insurance number and steal my identity? Or what if you're a psycho killer who just wants my address so you can come and kill me at night? You have not made a rational, reasonable side of yourself apparent before now.

T. GUY: Are you afraid to open it? Are you hiding more stolen merchandise in that wallet?

ABBY: I HAVE NOT STOLEN ANYTHING SINCE GRADE FOUR!

T. GUY: So! You don't deny a pattern of theft in your past!

ABBY: Gummy bears! Once! Jar and all! Once! No pattern!

T. GUY: Look lady, let's just get this all sorted out so we can get on with our lives. I don't like you. I don't like you at all. I don't like you in my store, I don't like you with your stuff spread all over my floor. I don't want you here at all. So let's just get on with this?

ABBY: *(holding out the wallet)* Take it!

TOUGH GUY takes wallet and opens it. Inside are a million cards.

T. GUY: Visa. Amex. Buyers Mart Platinum Card— good choice. MasterCard. Sears, Zellers and the Bay. Safeway, Superstore, Rogers Video. Three frequent coffee cards from three different places— no loyalty these days. Air

	Miles, bank card, phone card, Alberta health care, birth certificate, library card, Chapters discount card and driver's license.
	So where do we go from here, *(looking at driver's license)* Abigail Adams?
ABBY:	I go home, and write a letter to the manager. You go home and think about what else you could do for a living.
T. GUY:	I have to choose here. To believe you, or to not believe you. To take your word about the conditioner incident, against my better judgment, or to move into a more serious investigation.
ABBY:	Are you insane? What don't you get? I am not a criminal. You are not a cop. I have stolen nothing. You have to let me go. That is the only choice.
T. GUY:	I just don't know if I believe you. I may not have proof, but I know a thief in my guts. I see it in the back of your eyes.
ABBY:	NUT BAR!!!! Mr. Nut Bar, why don't you call the cashier and find out? I am getting the hell out of here . . . and I am going to complain—a lot.

ABBY has gathered up her belongings, and TOUGH GUY is barring the way.

T. GUY:	Abigail, I'm going to let you go today, against my better judgment. I can see that this has frightened you, and that is good. Go now, and know that you are barred from this Buyers Mart for the next twelve months. If I see you here, I'll be forced to remove you from the premises and charge you with trespassing.

ABBY walks away. Twilight Zone music.

ABBY:	Madness. Madness and mayhem. A Madman. Unbelievable. And not my fault. Clearly not my fault. *(checks her watch)* My God. It's only three. Already the day is epically, horrifically bad and it is only half over.

ABBY begins to weave her way through racks and racks of clothes. It is almost like a choreographed dance. She feels everything, slowly getting sucked in by the shopping, as the monologue continues.

ABBY: I'm gonna meet Joy tonight for a drink, if I have to drag her kicking and screaming. She's great. Deeply unjoyful, though. Her parents seriously missed the boat there. They should have called her Glee, which has always had nasty overtones to my mind, but not Joy.

I can tell her anything, and she will always have a harsh and judgmental thing to say. I love that. Cracks me up. Someday we are going to open a website for life coaching, where we provide realistic therapy for sad-sack losers over the internet.

You know, good advice like—

JOY: He hits you. You got two choices, pack your bags and get the hell out or do a Farrah and set the bed on fire. Now suck it up and decide if you're getting the suitcase or the gasoline.

ABBY: Or—

JOY: You keep getting fired? Well, eight jobs and eight companies and the only consistent thing is you, I'd say you suck. You'd best try getting a personality, some discipline and perhaps an aptitude for something that could eventually be lucrative.

ABBY: That kind of thing. Not nice, but funny. And true. Of course it never occurs to us to lump ourselves in with the sad-sack losers. But tonight I really need the perfect outfit to pick apart the universe. Some serious body armor.

Otherwise I'm worried I'll break down and cry, and let's face it, our friends don't really want to deal with our tears. It upsets the equilibrium and makes everyone uncomfortable. Repress, repress, repress.

ABBY goes into the change room with a pair of red pants.

ABBY: Clown pants. It's tough. I always want red pants, but then worry that I look like a clown or a short fire engine in them. I don't feel so good about the red pants.

ABBY throws the pants over the door.

ABBY: The changing stalls in these places really make me want to shoplift. Alone with the merchandise, it's really tempting. Especially in the big department stores, like the Bay, where everything is so overpriced and you can never find anyone to help you. And it's always when I'm desperately trying to find some help that I am most tempted to go layer three bras and four pairs of panties and socks and a turtle neck under my clothes and march out. Just to be vindictive. I don't, of course, but sometimes I am sweating with the effort not to, and running out of the store.

ABBY is back in her old clothes.

ABBY: But the important thing is, I don't do it. I have extra-ordinary will power.

Back in the Shopaholics meeting.

ABBY: I love the "It's all about will power" thing. I have will power. I do. I go to work everyday even though some days I'd rather call in sick. I don't bite my nails or yell when arguing. That's will power. OK, so I have never really successfully quit smoking but the thing is, I don't really want to.

And you have will power. You are not here because of a lack of will. It is not just a lack of will power that got you all those bags, those closets, those overstocked kitchen cupboards! What is it?

A dream. A dream got you here.

But can you buy a dream?

Take my friend Cammy. She spends three thousand dollars on a bike. Twice. Because she needed a road bike and a cross-country bike. Thirty-five hundred dollars on skiing equipment. And the pièce de resistance, four hundred dollars on hiking boots. These are not Jimmy Choos or Manilo Blahniks, just some butt-ugly hiking boots.

But the thing is, she actually uses these things. So, she spends some cash, but to LIVE her dream, not buy it.

But me, I'm starting to figure out I was just trying to buy the dang thing. You know, buy the bike thinking I'll suddenly become a sporto, but never actually riding it.

Store music. A SALES GIRL comes towards ABBY, who is standing by a stall, empty-handed.

GIRL: Are you finding everything?

ABBY: Oh . . . Sure!

GIRL: Can I get you anything? A size or anything?

ABBY: Um . . . Maybe some good butt pants, if you can find some.

GIRL: Good butt pants?

ABBY: Ya know, some pants that give good butt? A little lift, a little sculpt, not so tight you see cottage cheese?

To audience.

ABBY: How hard is that? Doesn't every woman know what constitutes good butt pants?

The SALES GIRL comes over with a pair of brown tweed pants.

GIRL: Give these a try.

ABBY goes into the changing stall. Struggles into too-tight pants. Looks at herself.

ABBY: Hideous. Just plain hideous. Lumpy, tight, adds at least ten pounds. *(to salesgirl)* What size are these? I'm a six.

GIRL: They're an eight.

ABBY: Oh . . . They look like crap. These are not butt pants. Maybe bad butt pants, But not good butt pants.

ABBY throws the pants over, they disappear.

ABBY: What about jeans? Got any jeans? I'd give some jeans a whirl if they gave good butt.

A pair of jeans fly over.

GIRL: I think you'll really like these. They're super low-rise flares, very fashion-forward.

ABBY tries them on. They are way too long in the leg and her belly rolls unflatteringly over the top.

ABBY: What the hell is this? Who the heck thought these ones up? Cut a girl off at the fattest part of herself, draw attention to the short legs? These are very bad for the butt, the belly, the legs. Get me something that gives me legs and holds my belly in, not displays it on a shelf!

To audience.

ABBY: My legs have always been a problem. As has been the belly. I didn't know this for the longest time, seven years to be exact. I was seven when my mom said I couldn't have the private plié lessons.

MOM: Maybe we could look into tap. It might lean down your short stubbies.

ABBY: So a paranoia is born.

Finally a last pair goes over the edge. Brown leather boot-cut pants.

GIRL: If these aren't good butt pants, I'll cut the hide into tortillas and eat them.

ABBY: Leather pants? You've got to be kidding? Who do you think I am, Britney flippin' Spears? Geez. All right, for a laugh.

ABBY tries them on. She does a take. She must look seriously, undeniably hot in these pants.

ABBY: Oh. My. God. I am hot. I am sex on legs, dangerous to know and inspiring hate in all other women. You want me, but don't know if you could take me! I am strong and powerful, encased in body armor! I am a dating warrior! I am a goddess!!!

GIRL: So the pants are good?

ABBY: Oh my god. I think I need a smoke.

ABBY emerges from the dressing room. She has the pants in hand. SALES GIRL is at the till.

GIRL: Do you need a top or anything with that?

ABBY: All I need is the pants. All I have ever needed is these pants.

GIRL: Some socks?

ABBY: Just get me the pants.

GIRL: That'll be five hundred and thirty one, ninety nine, with tax.

ABBY nearly dies.

ABBY: Five hundred and thirty two dollars? For some pants? For some dead cow? That is rent. A cheap seat to London. You must be mad!

GIRL: So no on the pants?

ABBY: Damn right that's a no! What the hell right do you have to charge that kind of money? You should be ashamed of yourself!

ABBY starts to walk out

GIRL: Too bad. Cuz your butt was killer in those pants.

ABBY freezes, turns around.

ABBY: Bag 'em.

ABBY walks out with bag in hand. We hear the sound of her heart beating incredibly fast, her breath coming in labored pants, faster, and faster and faster. Finally ABBY finds a wall in the mall and slides down it, crouching with her head between her knees. Silence.

ABBY: Six hundred dollars in the bank account. Five hundred dollars in overdraft. Eleven hundred dollars in total. Minus five hundred and thirty two dollars cow hide. Five hundred and thirty two dollars in cowhide! Leaving five hundred and sixty eight dollars. But really only sixty-eight dollars, because five hundred is overdraft. But today is the thirtieth, which means tomorrow I get paid. So fifteen hundred goes back in, bringing the false, overdraft free total back to fifteen hundred and sixty eight dollars, two thousand and sixty eight in spendable stuff, including the overdraft. But the day after tomorrow is the first. Which means—seven hundred dollars in rent.

ABBY pulls out phone bill.

ABBY: A hundred and fifty dollars on the land line. A hundred and seventy five dollars on the cell phone. Thirty dollars utilities. Forty dollars cable. Forty dollars cable internet. Thirty five dollars Alberta Health care. Crap, upped the premiums, forty dollars. Twenty dollars apartment insurance. Fifty dollars health club. Three hundred and fifty dollars on the MasterCard. Two hundred and seventy five dollars on the Visa. Thirty dollars on the Bay card. For a total of—Oh shit, and hundred dollars to Joy for Cammy's birthday present. For a total of—two thousand dollars. Which leaves me with . . . sixty eight dollars to eat, drink and be merry for the next two weeks. That's plenty. That's like five dollars a day for eating and drinking. That's fine.

               Except for . . . NINE DOLLARS FOR SMOKES! I'll just jump the LRT for free and hope that I don't get caught. I could even put some groceries on a card.

One lean two-week period, and then I get paid again. So I could do a little shopping now, and pay off the cards with the middle of the month paycheque.

ABBY spots someone. A MAN. The One that Got Away. ABBY tries to hide. Tries to scrunch up really small. Tries to run away. Tries to ignore his approach. Finally settles for sticking a cigarette in her mouth and pretending to look really hard for a place to smoke it.

THE ONE: Abigail?

ABBY: *(turning to look anywhere but at him)* Hmmm?

THE ONE: Abby!

ABBY: Hellooo? *(as though she can't see him}*

THE ONE: Abby, it's me—

ABBY: It's You! The miserable git who broke my heart, cheated on me with my high school nemesis, and left me for her and your love-child. It's you, who aside from all that was the best boyfriend I ever had, and who I still dream about with alarming regularity.

His voice goes back to normal.

THE ONE: It's me.

ABBY: Wow! You! How great to see you! How great!

THE ONE: Yeah, you look great.

ABBY: You look great.

THE ONE: Shopping?

ABBY: Actually, no. These aren't for me. Not really shopping much these days at all.

THE ONE: Really?

ABBY: No. Actually shopping too much. But that's because . . . because . . .

THE ONE:	You can't stop?
ABBY:	No! It 's because as well as my high-powered job in the marketing firm, I have my own business. A personal-shopping firm. It's actually more of a whole-lifestyle concept, because I shop for people and I also provide life coaching. And I teach yoga. Actually I don't even really shop much any more, I am so busy with my husband and two adorable children, and entertaining in my large Elbow Park home.
	(to the audience) My inside voice was saying that. My outside voice just said *(to him)*—ha ha ha.
THE ONE:	Still in administration?
ABBY:	*(to the audience)* I love that he calls reception administration. Like it matters more. *(to him)* Actually, in marketing.
THE ONE:	Wasn't it always a marketing firm?
ABBY:	Oh yes. But I've been promoted, I'm an assistant accounts rep. Well, the assistant to an accounts rep. But he really depends on me. On my ideas. My ideas on shopping.
THE ONE:	Good for you Abby! I think that's great. You were always too smart to waste your life answering phones.
ABBY:	Don't I know it . . . And you?
THE ONE:	Pretty good. I'm just back for a bit, visiting my folks and my son, and then I'm back off to London.
ABBY:	So London has really panned out for you, eh?
THE ONE:	Yeah, I really love it.
ABBY:	But Malcolm's not in London?
THE ONE:	Nice that you remember his name . . .
ABBY:	Oh yes, I remember.

THE ONE:	Nope, he's with his mom.
ABBY:	Oh. She isn't in London?
THE ONE:	We're separated.
ABBY:	Oh.
THE ONE:	And you?

Pause.

ABBY:	Oh, I've never really managed to successfully hook up with anyone after you. Everyone else was always too short or too dumb or not kind enough. Or I worried that they would be so sweet on the outside, and turn out to be a raging asshole like yourself, who cheated on me, got some girl knocked up and left me for her.
THE ONE:	And you?
ABBY:	Oh, I thought I'd answered you. You know, outside, inside voices and all that. Me, I'm great.
THE ONE:	Single?
ABBY:	Oh yes. Marriage and babies and stuff, that happens to other girls, not to me. I'm far too sane to sign my life over to another human being.
THE ONE:	Well, I'm sure you won't be able to stay single long.
ABBY:	Oh, I seem to manage.
THE ONE:	Well the men just must be crazy, not to be all over you.
ABBY:	Oh, they can get all over me, just not with the benefit of matrimony. *(to the audience)* Oh my god, now I sound like a slut. Great.

Pause.

ABBY:	But London is good?

THE ONE: Yeah. I mean, I'm based in London, but I'm really all over the place.

ABBY: Event planning?

THE ONE: Yeah.

ABBY: I can't believe you make a killing throwing parties all over Europe.

THE ONE: Pretty much. There's more of course, but kind of. You know, I'm thinking of starting my own firm. Risky, but I really think I could do it.

ABBY: Great! I am so sure you could.

THE ONE: Hey! While I'm in town maybe we could grab lunch and chat? With all your marketing experience maybe you could give me some ideas?

ABBY: You betcha. That would be great. You can just call me at the office.

THE ONE: Do you have a card?

ABBY: You know, I am all out. How 'bout you just use the phone book?

THE ONE: Great.

ABBY: Great.

THE ONE: Monday?

ABBY: Great.

THE ONE: It was really good to run into you, Abby.

ABBY: It was great.

THE ONE: So, we'll see you on Monday.

ABBY: You betcha. See ya . . .

She waves to him.

ABBY: I love him. He smells the same, like . . . I don't know what like, I've never met anyone else who smelled like that. When he knocked Kirsten up he tried to convince me it was all a mistake, a big error, that he loved me, but had to be a parent to this child, this LOVE child, and wouldn't I just allow him to love us both, me and this unborn child. Thank God for Joy, otherwise I would have caved completely.

JOY appears in a spotlight of Memory.

JOY: What a moron! What kind of idiot does he take you for? And with your nemesis, for Pete's sake. Like you would ever let his philandering hands near you again. What a pathetic loser.

Pause.

JOY: You do know that to take him back would not only be bad for you, but also a step back for womankind, right?

JOY fades away.

ABBY: God, it's hard to be a responsible representative for womankind. It seems to involve a lot of not eating, not crying and not sleeping with the men you'd really like to shutup.

Oh my god. I have to have lunch with him. I have to talk to him and not choke or cry or yell or throw things or throw myself at him. Thank god for the leather pants. They will hold me up, hold me in, keep my ass off the ground and my eye on the prize. What is the prize? What is the point? What does one wear with leather pants? Boots. One definitely wears little ankle booties with killer poke-your-eye out heels. The kind of boots that make your butt and boobs stick out. Right. Gotta buy boots. I gotta get the outfit that'll make me the girl he never gets over.

Back in the Shopaholics meeting.

ABBY: As you all know, the problem with trying to cut back on the shopping is there is always a real good reason to buy. More reason even than Christmas or a birthday or a sale. There is always some thin but valid excuse as to why you can't stop this week. Shopping is never the problem, always the solution. Too late you start to figure out that it is neither. It is a chronic symptom of something else, something much more wrong. Couldn't tell you what that is, you'll need a shrink for that, as it seems to vary from person to person, this deeply wrong thing.

                I knew that buying anything else would blow my already precarious budget. But I was investing in my future! If I had the right outfit, the planets aligned and my heart chakra was spinning, maybe The One and I would patch things up. Fall in love. Have great sex and move to London. Own a successful event-slash-life-planning business and two kids and a great Georgian town house in Kensington. And we would be able to do everything we wanted to and pay our bills on time.

                So I needed the boots. This falling in love, and all the subsequent emotional and financial stability, it would hinge on those leather pants and the perfect boots. I was about to invest in my future.

A small glowing light appears on the stage floor. In the puddle of light are a pair of killer leather ankle boots. Shiny. Beautifully brown. High sharp heels. They glow. As the light expands and expands, we see ABBY. She is transfixed by the boots. ABBY walks over to them. She steps into them. Some kind of fantastic sound cue. She is complete. ABBY struts downstage, pulls out a credit card. Silence except for her breath, and the little bleeping sounds that credit-card machines make when they are dialing up. A long beep, and then a booming voice.

VOICE: Rejected.

We hear her amplified heart rate. Her heart beats quickly. ABBY's breath catches. ABBY pulls out another card.

Silence except for her breath, and the little bleeping sounds. A long beep, and then a booming voice.

VOICE: Rejected.

We hear her amplified heart rate. ABBY pulls out a final card. The little bleeping sounds. A long beep, and then a booming voice.

VOICE: Rejected.

A total silence. Suddenly exploding into a cacophony of sound. Music from all the stores cutting in and out. Cash registers dinging, etc.

MR. BANKS: You appear to have an income.

GIRL: That'll be five hundred and thirty one, ninety nine, with tax.

TOUGH GUY: Are you hiding stolen merchandise in that wallet?

GRANDMA: Abby, you will never be a pretty girl—

MR. BANKS: You really need the cards.

CASH GIRL: Hold on a sec, the conditioner is two for the same price, do you want another one?

T. GUY: I don't like you. I don't like you at all. I don't want you here at all.

LINDA: Great. You must be really pleased with yourself. That must feel really good.

T. GUY: I can see that this has frightened you, and that is good. You need to be frightened.

GRANDMA: Don't disappoint folks, Abby.

THE ONE: It's me.

JOY: You'd best try getting a personality, some discipline and perhaps an aptitude for something that could eventually be lucrative.

MR. BANKS: Possibly.

GIRL: Give these a try.

T. GUY: Don't deny a pattern!

JOY: What kind of idiot does he take you for?

T. GUY: It is not too late to change your life, and I hope you use this chance to do just that.

JOY: You do know that to take him back would not only be bad for you, but also a step back for womankind, right?

THE ONE: You were always too good to spend your life as a— *(reverb, echoing boom)* —spoiled, compulsive shopaholic.

ABBY collapses. ABBY blacks out, straight down in the floor, as the SALES GIRL hovers over her.

GIRL: Can you hear me? Are you OK?

ABBY: Mom?

GIRL: You've just fallen.

ABBY: What happened?

GIRL: I'm going to get you some water. You just sit tight.

The SALES GIRL disappears to get some water. ABBY tries to stand up. She is unsteady on her feet. ABBY leaves the store, weaving away, just as The SALES GIRL comes out with the water. The SALES GIRL sees her leaving, shrugs, and drinks that water herself as she exits the stage.

Shift back to the Shopaholics meeting.

ABBY: When I was a little girl, I never wanted to be a princess, or a figure skater, or even a ballerina, for all the longing for tutus and perfect pliés. I always wanted to be an astronaut, or a president or Indiana Jones. When I played Star Wars with the kids on the block, I always made Richie Noland play Princess Leah, so I could be Darth Vader. I couldn't wait to grow up and be in charge of things. Instead I somehow ended up charging things and being in charge of . . . nothing.

So. Black Friday, which ended up being Good Friday, the first Friday of the rest of my life.

We see JOY cutting the cards. ABBY hands them to her, one by one.

ABBY: What will I do in the case of an emergency?

JOY shoots her a look, and cuts the Visa. ABBY scrambles around, picking up the pieces. JOY holds out her hand for the Amex. ABBY is weeping. ABBY is very slow to hand it over, finally JOY snatches it.

JOY: Don't be a baby! This was your idea.

But this one is not a clean cut, JOY really has to hack and fold, fold and hack, to break that one down. By this time ABBY is hyperventilating.

JOY: Now give me the MasterCard.

ABBY: Noooooo!!!! I can't! I can't do it! I'll be naked! Defenseless! Without hope or help or a way out of a stinky third world country if I get kidnapped—

JOY: Give it to me.

ABBY: No.

JOY: Hand it over.

ABBY: I need something for emergencies.

JOY: How will you decide what's an emergency?

ABBY: PLEASE!

JOY: Fine. For emergencies. Go get me a Tupperware container. With some water in it.

ABBY exits the stage and gets a bowl of water. She re-enters with it. She is puzzled.

JOY: Put the card in the water.

ABBY: What?

JOY: JUST DO IT!

ABBY puts the card in the water.

JOY: Put the lid on the bowl!

ABBY puts the lid on the bowl.

JOY: Now I will go and put this in the freezer. And you will have to think long and hard, as long as it takes for the ice to melt, about declaring a state of emergency and using this card.

JOY exits the stage. Back to the Shopaholics meeting.

ABBY: I headed into the weekend with no credit cards. No shopping planned. Just . . . me.

                 It's been forty-five days. And let me tell you, I don't really remember the first forty-eight hours. All the hours blur together, because even now I think, well, you made it through that last hour. Here comes the next.

                 I did meet him. For lunch. And it was OK. We talked. He's a nice man. Screwed-up big time, but a nice man. Joy made me take back the pants. So I went sans body armor. I wasn't dressed like The Girl He Would Never Forget. Just like . . . me.

                 Cammy assured me that my earn-more-spend-less idea was actually fairly sound, so I've asked them to train and promote me at work. We'll see. They said they needed to think it over and we'll talk about it in my performance review.

                 I asked for one after my first meeting with a life coach. Funny, seeing one instead of being one. And I might be one one day, but right now, I got a lot of stuff to sort out.

                 So here I am.

                 And I have absolutely no idea what's going to happen to me ten minutes from now. I have no idea about tomorrow, or the next day, or the day after that.

I know folks always tell us that you can't buy happiness. And I know, they are right. Even when I was buying stuff, I knew that was pretty much true.

But you can buy endorphins. And sedatives, and five-minute confidence boosters. The only thing is, it's like leprechaun gold. You turn around twice and it's gone.

And I am finding it pretty hard to be a grown up. To be responsible and think and feel and stuff. I don't know why it's so hard being a grown up, I don't remember being a kid being a laugh a minute either. I'm trying to be really brave. And honest. And I'm scared a lot. Scared of doing things instead of buying them. Scared of healing instead of buying band aids, scared of yelling and crying and laughing instead of shopping.

And I reckon, I'll be OK. You'll be OK. There's a self help book in there somewhere.

So. There you have it. The first meeting of the first chapter of Shopaholics Known. I hope I see you again. I hope you tell your story next time. My parting shots of wisdom— Freeze the credit card. Take it one hour at a time. Don't buy the pants. Go forth into the world empty-handed.

Go forth into the world with your hands outstretched. When your hands are empty of all the things you don't really need, there just might be room for the stuff you do need. And I wanna make sure that when the good stuff comes, I'm ready to grab it.

The circle of light gets smaller and smaller on ABBY until it is close in on her empty hands, outstretched. Blackout.

End of play.

Borrow Me

By Clem Martini

Borrow Me was commissioned directly for the stage by
Lunchbox Theatre. It premiered January 13, 1997 at
Lunchbox Theatre, Calgary, with the following cast.

SHARON BENNET	Barbara Gates Wilson
RUSSEL BENNET	David LeReaney
JENNY AMBROGIANO	Shawna Lori Burnett
GORDON MENZIES	Joe-Norman Shaw

Directed by John Cooper

Set Design by Witek Wisniewski

Costumes by Amber Humphries

Lighting Design by Cimmeron Meyer

Stage Manager: Susan McNeil

Borrow Me was originally workshopped as part of the Petro-Canada
Stage One Plays in April, 1995 with Donna Belleville (Sharon),
Terry Belleville (Russel), Enid Ray Adams (Jenny), and Martin Evans
(Gordon). The workshop was directed by Kevin McKendrick.

Characters

SHARON BENNET

RUSSEL BENNET

JENNY AMBROGIANO

GORDON MENZIES

The very pleasant dining room of RUSSEL and SHARON. At the rear of the dining room we can see a lovely patio leading out onto a deck. It is early evening and the sky as seen through the windows is a darkening blue. RUSSEL and SHARON are setting their table for dinner. They move in and out of the room as they make their preparations, continuing to converse throughout the entire operation. JENNY—Russel's young friend—stands with a drink in her hand, watching.

SHARON:	Do you think we should call someone?
RUSSEL:	No. Have you chilled the wine?
SHARON:	Yes. He should have been back forty minutes ago.
RUSSEL:	Who do you suggest we call? His mother?
SHARON:	The police or something.
RUSSEL:	Right, let's alert Interpol—
SHARON:	—He could be lost. It could be something serious—
RUSSEL:	—It's not.—
SHARON:	—He's taken the entire week off since his accident, you know. The entire week—
RUSSEL:	Only in your books could taking the week off be equated with serious. And speaking of both books and lost, have you seen my date book?
SHARON:	No.
RUSSEL:	I was looking for it this afternoon—
SHARON:	—We can't wait much longer—

RUSSEL: —It's vanished.—

SHARON: —Everything's almost done.—

RUSSEL: —I can't find anything these days.—

SHARON: —Where could he have run to?—

RUSSEL: —First it's my date book—

SHARON: —I should phone *someone*—

RUSSEL: —My electronic note pad.—

SHARON: —911 seems a bit drastic—

RUSSEL: —And now my best friend's misplaced. It's annoying. Here Jen.

JENNY accepts a fresh drink from RUSSEL.

RUSSEL: Make yourself useful.

JENNY: OK.

RUSSEL exits. JENNY looks about. RUSSEL returns.

JENNY: How?

RUSSEL: How do you normally make yourself useful?

JENNY: I'm an actor. Normally I'm pretending I'm something I'm not.

Exit RUSSEL.

JENNY: Like useful.

Enter SHARON.

JENNY: Is there anything I can do?

SHARON: I think everything is just about set.

JENNY drinks.

JENNY: Whew. That's a . . . powerful drink. He always make drinks this powerful?

SHARON:	I wouldn't know, he never makes them for me. Russel? Should we do something?
RUSSEL:	He's a grown up.
SHARON:	But he hasn't seemed the same since he got here—
RUSSEL:	He's fine.
SHARON:	He's definitely not himself.
RUSSEL:	He's *fine.*
SHARON:	And I don't like the look of the weather. It's getting windy.
JENNY:	And dark.

Enter RUSSEL.

RUSSEL:	"Dark"? Dark doesn't constitute weather.
JENNY:	No, but it constitutes . . . what's . . . out there.

RUSSEL exits.

JENNY:	I'll do something. If there's something for me to do.

SHARON exits.

JENNY:	Or, I can stand here and drink. All in favor. Aye. Motion passed.

JENNY turns, looks out the window and screams.

JENNY:	Ah!
RUSSEL:	What?

Enter GORDON.

JENNY:	Your friend's arrived. I think.
RUSSEL:	And just in the nic'o'time too. There's nothing that offends Sharon's middle-class sensibilities more than someone late to dinner. She was about ready to release the hounds.

SHARON: I was worried. Sue me.

SHARON gives GORDON, who seems a little lost in his own thoughts, a quick hug.

SHARON: Must've been some run.

RUSSEL: Aw, he hasn't been running, look at him, he's not sweating.

SHARON: He's fit. Unlike you.

RUSSEL: What? He's so fit he can run an hour and half without sweating? He's been to the bar. Check his breath.

SHARON: Just because he doesn't smoke a pack before he gargles in the morning. How was the run?

GORDON stands still—apparently smelling the air.

SHARON: Gordon?

GORDON: Sorry I'm late. I got turned around in the woods back there. It smells, *great*, in here. Can I do anything?

RUSSEL: "Can I do anything?" You gotta love a guy who can say that with a straight face.

RUSSEL pinches GORDON's cheek.

RUSSEL: The table's set, food's on, and he asks, "Can I do anything?" Isn't that another way of asking, "Can I eat?"

SHARON: Gordon, this is Jenny Ambrogiano. Jenny, this is our very good friend, Gordon Menzies. Jenny is a very talented actress who has appeared in a number of Russel's films including his latest.

GORDON: Pleased to meet you.

JENNY: I've heard so much about you already.

GORDON: Good or bad?

GORDON removes the lid from one of the dishes and inhales deeply.

JENNY: Bit of both.

RUSSEL: I've tried to warn her. Ah, there's nothing like someone
           else going for a brisk run to sharpen my appetite.

*GORDON continues relishing the aroma of the dish—he almost sticks his
entire head in the bowl—and bathes his face in the steam.*

RUSSEL: You OK, buddy?

GORDON: It smells really . . . *really*, great in here.

RUSSEL: Yeah, that would be the cooking.

Slight pause.

RUSSEL: You want to freshen up or anything?

GORDON: No, I didn't work up much of a sweat—You're right, I
           didn't run, I ended up walking. There's so much to look
           at.

RUSSEL: To look at?

GORDON: Yeah, it's, *wonderful,* out there.

RUSSEL: Right, right. There're the trees . . . *(glances out the window)*
           . . . and, ah, a lot more trees. OK. Well, sit down, I'm
           starved. So, Gordo, for dinner tonight we have Almond
           Gai Ding, almond and asparagus, diced carrots and
           almonds, marzipan for dessert, and in case anyone needs
           anything to snack on later, we have roasted almonds.

GORDON: In that case, I guess I'll have some almonds.

SHARON: Russel! Stop it—he's joking. Gordon is allergic to almonds,
           he had a really awful incident just a few weeks ago.

RUSSEL: Tell Jen how.

GORDON: No . . .

RUSSEL: Tell her! OK, I'll tell her—he can't touch almonds, *must
           not* touch almonds, and he's romancing some girl, has his
           tongue so far down her throat he can taste her shoe size—

SHARON: —He was kissing her.

RUSSEL: —And *suddenly* he feels this tingling in his tongue, among other places, so he disengages his tongue, among other things—

SHARON: —He *asks* her "Have you had any almonds?" —

RUSSEL: —And *she* asks, "Why, does my breath smell?"—as if that would be it, right? I mean, how often does someone tell you you *reek* of almonds?—

SHARON: —It turns out she *has* had almonds, just a couple of hours before.—

RUSSEL: —That was all it took. Another beautiful relationship ruined by what was consumed earlier that day. Imagine her surprise, eh? I mean, you stay away from onions, garlic, fish—sure—but almonds?

              Wine!

RUSSEL jumps up and exits to the kitchen. GORDON again seems lost in his own thoughts.

JENNY: So? What happened?

GORDON: Oh. I almost died.

SHARON: *Did* die. Clinically dead, heart stopped, no respiration. Ten minutes. Isn't that amazing?

RUSSEL reappears carrying a wine bottle and a big book.

RUSSEL: There we go. And there you go.

RUSSEL throws GORDON the book.

RUSSEL: You want some?

JENNY: Ah . . .

JENNY appears undecided, then gulps down her remaining drink.

JENNY: Sure.

RUSSEL: I didn't mean you had to knock back your other one.

JENNY: Well, it was getting, stale. The book, is . . .

RUSSEL: It's a dictionary.

JENNY: A dictionary? I see.

She doesn't. JENNY looks at the others who seem to find this literary addition normal.

JENNY: We're, improving our word power over dinner?

SHARON: For years we've gotten together for dinner and played a game called Dictionary. Here's your piece of paper and pencil.

RUSSEL: He picks a word that nobody knows the definition of, and then writes down the real definition, and, a made-up one.

SHARON: Everyone writes down their own definition, hands it in, and then we try to guess what the real one is.

RUSSEL: See? We eat. We play. We talk. It's very civilized.

GORDON has apparently discovered his soup.

RUSSEL: Gordon?

GORDON: This soup is *very* good. *Very.*

RUSSEL: Thanks, I thought for a moment you'd expired.

GORDON: I've got my word.

RUSSEL: Shoot.

GORDON: Lapidate. Anyone know it?

SHARON: Not me.

RUSSEL: Nope.

Pause.

JENNY: No.

RUSSEL: So, that's the word. Write down your definition.

GORDON: I'll have some more of that soup.

RUSSEL: There are *more* dishes to come, you know. Pace yourself. It's like a triathalon, appetizer, main course *and* dessert.

JENNY: I don't know it.

RUSSEL: Right. None of us know it.

JENNY: Right. Can I have the book to look it up?

RUSSEL: No. Jenny. *He's* going to tell us what the definition is *after*. So write down your definition, your made-up definition.

JENNY: Right. OK, OK. Now I get it. I say it's a Roman soldier.

RUSSEL: *No*, you don't tell us. You *write it down*. Hand it in. We read it aloud. And then we guess. You're trying to fool us. Right? For points.

Pause.

RUSSEL: Actors. You see why we have to give them a script to work from?

SHARON: It's her first time.

JENNY: O-kay. Now I get it. I write it down.

RUSSEL: You write it down.

JENNY: You've done this a lot then?

RUSSEL: Played it for over fifteen years.

JENNY: Wow. *Fifteen years*? Wow! I didn't know you all went back *that* far.

RUSSEL: This guy taught it to me. And Sharon and Gord were going together before I came on the scene so Lord knows what he taught her.

JENNY: Wow. So, you two married after that, eh? That's almost like, incest or something, isn't it?

93

RUSSEL: Just like. OK, there's my answer.

SHARON: He's got mine already.

JENNY: And that's mine. I guess.

RUSSEL: Read 'em out.

GORDON: Lapidate: To go out with someone of the opposite sex and spend most of the evening on their lap.

RUSSEL: Who wrote that?

GORDON: Lapidate: To discover the age of an archaeological find through the use of ultrasound. Lapidate: A Greek soldier. Lapidate: A family of marsupials found in the south pacific. Lapidate: To stone someone to death.

RUSSEL: You're not reading the right ones. No one wrote, "To stone someone to death."

GORDON: "To stone someone to death."

RUSSEL: Someone not sleeping well nights? I say it's the fourth one.

SHARON: Second one.

JENNY: Third one.

RUSSEL: Can't vote for your own, Jen.

JENNY: Oh. How did you know it was mine?

RUSSEL: Roman soldier? Greek soldier? You see a pattern there?

JENNY: Oh. Fourth I guess then.

GORDON: I get two points for fooling everyone. The answer is: "To stone someone to death."

RUSSEL: No? That's a word? I get a point; the ultrasound thing was mine. Did you write that horrible sitting on someone's lap for a date definition?

SHARON: Yes.

RUSSEL: Hang your head in shame. Then the marsupials thing must be yours too.

GORDON: Yeah.

RUSSEL: Three points! And the big guy leaps into the lead.

SHARON: Pass me the book.

The book moves to SHARON.

RUSSEL: Now, the truth. You didn't actually walk anywhere, did you? You went for an espresso.

GORDON: Just walked.

RUSSEL: Where?

GORDON drains the rest of his soup directly from the bowl.

GORDON: Hah. I'll take a smidgen more. Up the hill. It's gorgeous. Near the top, there's a place that overlooks the city. Ever been there?

RUSSEL: Who knows? The city's situated in a valley. There're a lot of places that are bound to overlook it. Hills, valleys, you know, it's that altitude thing.

GORDON: It's got a bench.

SHARON: You know the one—

GORDON: You must've been there once.

RUSSEL: I may have been there. Lotta benches, lotta paths in this world.

The door to the kitchen suddenly slams shut.

RUSSEL: What the hell was that?

RUSSEL rises to examine the door. He opens it.

RUSSEL: The pressure changes in this valley are a bitch.

RUSSEL closes it, opens it. It doesn't appear to stick.

SHARON: I've been up there with you. Russ, you've been there—it's the one with that big rock.

GORDON: That's it.

RUSSEL: OK, that one. Yeah, I've been up there. I just didn't catch which one.

GORDON: That's because you never pay attention to me, Russ.

RUSSEL: What?

Pause.

RUSSEL: What did you say?

GORDON: I said you never pay attention to me. Why?

RUSSEL: No reason. I thought you . . . said something else.

Slight pause.

RUSSEL: Um. I should bring on the, ah. I'll fetch out the main course.

RUSSEL exits.

JENNY: You two were childhood sweeties, then?

SHARON: Not quite that far. We were all in university together.

JENNY: Cool. You rich?

GORDON: Ah, no. I do all right.

SHARON: Gordon is a podiatrist.

JENNY: Ohhhh, it must be so *great* working with kids—

SHARON: That's, feet—

GORDON and SHARON simultaneously correct Jenny.

GORDON: Feet, actually—

JENNY: —Oh, right—

GORDON: —Pod not ped—

JENNY: —Sure, yeah, of course. I just figure these are things I should ask. Your income, your hobbies, your shoe size—I think Russel invited me out to complete the foursome, which kinda makes me your blind dinner date. Without either of us actually being blind.

JENNY laughs immoderately at this, recovers and drinks.

SHARON: Jenny's the lead in Russel's latest production.

JENNY: Yeah, and he says he's got another in the works that's a little more—

JENNY indicates something weighty.

JENNY: —and still right up my alley.

GORDON: What sort of film is this one?

JENNY: Action. It's my—

JENNY gestures.

JENNY: —these days. There's this performer's boarding school in the woods for wayward girls? And this guy who arrives to scout us out turns out instead to be a crazed psychopathic killer, I crawl semi-nude through the swamp and finally snap his neck with a dead fall arrangement I construct from the torn remnants of my bra. You gotta love a happy ending, right?

GORDON: Yeah.

SHARON: Yeah.

JENNY: The great thing is that although it's kinda geared at that slasher/stalker/serial killer/teen wet dream mentality that's a little bit ooey, it's got this subversive feminist message running under it because after all my character has got the, you know, ingenuity, to save herself from the bad guy with nothing but her brains and a slinky push up brassiere.

JENNY's elbow slips off the table. She recovers.

JENNY: I think that's commendable.

RUSSEL: *(from the kitchen)* Here it comes.

SHARON taps GORDON on the elbow.

SHARON: When I heard about your accident, I convinced Russel to prepare your favorite dish.

JENNY: Cool. Which is?

GORDON: Ah.

SHARON: Gordon?

RUSSEL enters.

RUSSEL: Lamb.

GORDON: Lamb! Of course.

RUSSEL unveils the roast lamb.

JENNY: Oooh.

SHARON: Russel is very big on presentation.

RUSSEL: If it doesn't *look* good, it might just as well be crap, you know.

SHARON: So, it's just as well for us that it *looks* good, right?

RUSSEL: And for each operation one must have the correct instruments, right Doc? Luckily, I have at my disposal, a *Christmas gift* from my wife—

RUSSEL produces a carving knife.

RUSSEL: —a knife.

SHARON: Tsk. He's always complained that the knives we owned weren't any good—

RUSSEL: —But not just *any* knife—

SHARON: —They were too dull—

RUSSEL: —No, no, this knife—part of a spectacular *set* of knives— is built to such exacting standards, forged in Copenhagen, strengthened with titanium, that I, mere knife-handling puppy that I am, feel barely qualified to wield the mighty instrument. Still, I will do my humble best.

SHARON: Soon, I hope. He makes such a fuss about everything.

RUSSEL: Knives. Now, is that romantic or what?

SHARON: It's what you asked for.

RUSSEL serves the lamb.

JENNY: If you two were best buddies, how did you end up with his girlfriend?

SHARON: I suppose Russel stole me away from Gordon.

RUSSEL: Oh oh. That's your story.

SHARON: That's the way it was.

RUSSEL: Don't you believe it. Back then I couldn't steal anybody from anyone, I was just this poor little philosophy undergraduate, selling a little grass on the side, watching the world lift weights and getting sand kicked in my ego. The Commitment Meter was running, this guy didn't plug another coin in, and along I came. Like they say, there's one born every minute. Vegetable moussaka coming up.

RUSSEL exits.

SHARON: Russel has a wonderful way of making you feel very special at the precise moment that he wants something, and only then. I'm sure you'll learn that soon enough.

RUSSEL re-enters with side dishes.

RUSSEL: Now *this* guy—

RUSSEL pinches Gordon's cheek.

RUSSEL:	—back at university was very smooth. I mean, he made silk look like an emery board, I mean he slept with *everybody*.
SHARON:	Russel, you are so full of nonsense sometimes, Gordon had other things to do—
RUSSEL:	—We *all* had other things to do. We just didn't do 'em—
SHARON:	—Not everyone failed to complete university like you—
RUSSEL:	—Which you never let me forget. And a fat lot of good it would have done if I *had* completed my *philosophy* degree.
SHARON:	Philosophy is a respectable study, Russel, I got something out of the philosophy course I took. I mean, we all have our *own* personal philosophy to guide us—
RUSSEL:	—Excuse me. You have a philosophy?
SHARON:	Yes, I do, Russel.
RUSSEL:	I'm sorry, Sharon, Shopping does not constitute a philosophy.
SHARON:	I'm not talking about shopping and you know it. Whenever I become, depressed, it is my *philosophy* which sustains me—
RUSSEL:	—And self-pity isn't a philosophy either, dear. Look, perhaps the one real thing any of us learned while at university was just how useless it all was.
SHARON:	It *wasn't* useless.
RUSSEL:	Course it was.
SHARON:	*Gordon* made use of his time there.
RUSSEL:	Absolutely! The best possible use of time—
SHARON:	—That's all I'm saying—

RUSSEL: —And that's all I'm saying. He made the best possible use of his time—He slept with everybody.

SHARON: He *didn't* sleep with everybody.

RUSSEL: He slept with you.

Long pause.

SHARON: I suppose it can be nice, under some circumstances, to be characterized as Everywoman.

Pause.

SHARON: Thanatos. That's my word. Does anyone know it?

JENNY: Not me.

JENNY finishes her drink and pours herself another.

GORDON: No.

RUSSEL: No.

They all write their answers.

SHARON: That's the word then. Everybody write down your answers. It looks like we've forgotten ice water, and we may end up needing some before the night's through, so maybe I'll fetch out a jug.

SHARON exits. Pause.

JENNY: You sold drugs?

RUSSEL: It was the eighties! Everyone sold drugs. Girl guides canvassed door to door with cookies and lines of coke.

GORDON: Does Russel present this cynical side of himself at work?

RUSSEL: It's not a side—it runs straight through. I mean, cynicism is *the* guiding philosophy of the new millennium, folks. The "paradigm," right? Good-bye Age of Aquarius, hello Age of Wal-Mart. Anyone who isn't a cynic in this day and age just hasn't grown up yet.

JENNY: I'm not cynical.

RUSSEL: Exactly. You're an actor, you're paid not to grow up.

JENNY: You just need to find the, the . . .

JENNY gestures.

JENNY: . . . the *good* in people.

RUSSEL: There may very well come a day when I *feel* for people and open up and embrace their, you know, humanity. You may be right. And when that day comes, Jenny—shoot me. OK? Just shoot me. I mean, OK, you take this drug thing, eh? The beginnings of my *incipient* cynicism, if you will, all right? It was a very middle-class operation I was running. Three tidy little bungalows with picket fences, basements chock fulla the latest hydroponics equipment, and thousands of these teeny little plants—you know, I believe I even received a government start-up grant to finance this initially, as part of an urban-renewal thingee. And my clientele were all very proper moms and dads with their own little bungalows—Anyway, I was doing wonderfully, as I'm sure you can imagine, and Gord can attest I threw great parties—*but*—the cops come by one night. Kick the door down. Do I know how deep I am in the blah blah blah? And how long *exactly* have I been illegally blah blah blah blah and I had just better *cooperate* and so on and so forth and ahhhh—

RUSSEL draws a long pull from his drink.

JENNY: So, what did you do?

RUSSEL puts his drink back on the table.

RUSSEL: What did I do? *Gave them their cut,* of course. *(he laughs)* Gave them their cut! That's all they ever wanted. Major epiphany, that. Give everyone their cut, put enough names on a payroll and you can turn the filthiest lucre ivory-snow white. I mean, what are your rum-runners of yesteryear but the corporate models of today, your crack dealers of today but the CEO's of tomorrow. *(takes another drink)* Anyway, it was just grass and the odd bit'a hash. It's like purchasing a starter home. You build up this little nest egg and then you turn it over. I turned it over into the film industry, which, really, apart from being legal bears an uncanny resemblance to selling drugs.

SHARON re-enters with water, sets it on the table, then picks up the slips of paper.

SHARON: Thanatos: A Greek flan made with tomatoes. Thanatos: A poison-throwing snail found in the Australian ocean. Thanatos: Death personified in Greek mythology. Thanatos: the act of digesting something either too large or too toxic for the system to fully process. Thanatos: A rare skin condition.

SHARON is finished. Slight pause.

JENNY: Could you read them again?

SHARON looks at the papers.

SHARON: Certainly. Thanatos . . . *(clears her throat)* Thanatos . . . *(pauses, but can't continue)* But first, perhaps I'll go to the washroom. You'll excuse me.

SHARON sets down the papers and exits. Slight pause.

RUSSEL: I suppose it falls to me as the designated married person to see if she's not feeling well. Excuse me. There's rice, and a savory tomato dish. Help yourself.

RUSSEL follows after SHARON. JENNY and GORDON sit at the table.

JENNY: Can I reflesh, that is refresh your drink?

GORDON: Certainly.

JENNY pours them both a drink.

GORDON: Could you pass me the tomatoes?

JENNY does so. GORDON takes many.

JENNY: You've got a hearty appetite. How old are you?

GORDON: Forty two. You?

JENNY: Twenty. And you were, all of you, back in university together, when?

GORDON: A decade and half or so.

JENNY: So, when you guys were all in university, I was . . . seven. It's kind of like I've suddenly been beamed back to a convention of my old babysitters—I mean you guys are cool, but the time lag on some of this stuff is pretty mega. You know? I mean when you guys were dating, or whatever, I was . . . watching the Teletubbies.

A silence falls between them.

JENNY: How did it feel?

GORDON: What?

JENNY: Being dead.

GORDON: You've probably heard it all. Bright light, long tunnel. All that.

JENNY: It was peaceful?

GORDON: Very.

JENNY: You look peaceful.

GORDON: Do I? I'm not. It's not easy coming back from the dead.

JENNY: Well, you *look* very peaceful. And if you can't be something the next best thing is to look something, right?

Slight pause

JENNY: Does everything . . . *(gestures)* . . . you know? . . . taste better?

GORDON: Yes. *(then after a moment's consideration . . .)* Yes. Everything does. Taste better. Smell better. Feel . . .

GORDON rubs his wine glass gently against his cheek. For a moment he is absolutely lost in that sensation.

GORDON: . . . better. It's quite a, surprise.

JENNY: I'd like that.

GORDON: Sure, although you've got a glass right there—

JENNY: No, I mean a second chance.

GORDON: Second chance? Excuse me, but . . . I wasn't aware that you were so very far down the road with your first chance.

JENNY laughs, but it's a laugh bereft of humor.

JENNY: Oh, I don't know about that. I don't know. Sometimes I think I am so far down the lane I can't remember putting the key in the ignition. You know?

GORDON: Yeah.

JENNY: You—are so lucky.

RUSSEL enters.

GORDON: Sharon will join us shortly. Lucky for what?

JENNY: His wicked near-death experience.

GORDON: Oh that. I heard the brain dumps tons of organic hallucinogens into your system whenever it seems you're likely to kick. Just the body's way of throwing a really bitching wrap party.

JENNY: Why?

GORDON: Pardon?

JENNY: What did you come back for?

Slight pause.

GORDON: There were still things I needed to do.

RUSSEL laughs.

RUSSEL: "Still things I needed to do"? Oh *pleeze.* I mean, I'll bet you didn't know, Jenny, that sitting among us was the Mother Theresa of Podiatry, a man drawn back, literally drawn back, *from the dead,* to ease the suffering of all those ailing, needy feet. You—

RUSSEL pinches GORDON's cheek.

RUSSEL: —are so fulla crap sometime. Jenny?

JENNY has fallen asleep.

GORDON: She's gone.

RUSSEL: Wow. No stamina, eh? Back when we were mere sprouts we'd dance, drink, do drugs, stay up forty hours straight and still screw like mink. And now the present generation has come to this sorry pass. I ask you, Gordo, what's the point of our suffering, striving, and finally achieving spectacular success at this late juncture if the party's just going to wind down.

GORDON finishes his drink. He lingers over the last drop. RUSSEL automatically moves to refill the glass. GORDON places the glass on the table.

GORDON: We've got to talk.

RUSSEL: Sure buddy. Bout what?

GORDON: Lapidation.

RUSSEL: What?

GORDON: About what happened up the hill.

RUSSEL: You mean when you went for your walk?

GORDON: No.

RUSSEL: Then what?

GORDON: I know, Russel.

RUSSEL: What?

GORDON: I know what happened up there.

JENNY wakes suddenly.

JENNY: A rare skin condition!

JENNY realizes that she is not playing Dictionary.

JENNY: Oh Russel honey, I've got to go to bed. I'm wasted.

RUSSEL: I'll walk you down. It won't take me more than a minute, she's staying at the old house. If you could tell Sharon. I'm not sure I understand what you're talking about, but we'll chat when I get back. OK?

GORDON: Sure.

GORDON leaves to tell Sharon. RUSSEL helps JENNY up.

JENNY: I'm sorry. I tried to be good, but I don't know what I'm doing here. I know you and she have got your own . . . arrangements, but I just feel so weird. Around your buddy, your wife.

JENNY collapses against RUSSEL.

JENNY: And I'm soooo hammered.

RUSSEL: That's what happens when you drink non-stop.

JENNY: And she just kept *looking* at me. You know?

RUSSEL: I know.

RUSSEL kisses JENNY.

JENNY: Are you mad?

RUSSEL: No.

They kiss again. Enter GORDON. RUSSEL and JENNY stop.

RUSSEL: I'll get your coat.

RUSSEL exits.

JENNY: He's sweet.

GORDON: Yeah.

JENNY: And like a, a mentor to me. We've been working together so long, and on this film, we've, the cast and everyone, just gotten real tight—

GORDON: —I know.

JENNY: It's like we're family.—

GORDON: —I know.

JENNY: It's not like what you might be thinking—

GORDON: —Believe me, I know. Believe me.

RUSSEL re-enters.

RUSSEL: We can go.

JENNY: It was nice meeting you.

GORDON: You take care.

RUSSEL and JENNY exit. GORDON stands and looks out the window. He plucks up a piece of lamb and pops it in his mouth. SHARON enters.

SHARON: So, what happened?

GORDON: Jenny had too much to drink. Russel's walking her back.

SHARON: She's very sweet, don't you think, in her own way? And very attractive. A remarkable actress, Russel says. He says he thinks she'll go far, I mean she already has. Ever since school you've represented something of a standard that Russel's felt he's had to live up to.

GORDON: Really?

SHARON: Oh yes. He's trying very hard tonight to impress you. With everything he's done, and everything he's got.

SHARON turns back to the table.

SHARON: Anyway, the food will get cold, we might as well eat. And would you like another drink? Russel has been working so much on the film lately it's nice to have company over. I get lonely since we built this new place. In a way I liked the old house, it's like there's no place for me here. Now, when no one else is with me I feel like I'm the security person hired to make the rounds. Check the corner. Check the hallway. Check the bedrooms—here's your drink—some nights I just *float* around from room to room to room like a ghost, I mean, I might as well be a ghost in my own home . . . boo!

SHARON leans in and kisses GORDON, then stops.

SHARON: That was nice. Is something wrong?

SHARON kisses GORDON again.

SHARON: Just like old times. What's the matter? You don't have to worry about Russel, you *know* he's involved with Jenny, or someone else, or Jenny *and* someone else. It's hard to keep track. Like I said, it's a very big house and a very big city and most films have very large casts, and he's a very, very active husband and with the guest house and all sometimes it can be kind of like playing the shell game on a very large scale.

GORDON: I know all about that.

SHARON: So whatever we do, won't be—are you all right?

GORDON draws away.

GORDON: I feel a little strange.

SHARON: Strange?

GORDON: Hot. And . . .

SHARON: What?

GORDON glances down.

GORDON: I have an erection.

Slight pause.

SHARON: Good. I mean . . . Then everything's working, normally, right?

SHARON approaches GORDON. He draws back.

GORDON: No.

SHARON: What?

GORDON: No. I'm forgetting, *everything.*

SHARON draws close and puts her arms around GORDON.

SHARON: Well. It seems to be coming back to you.

GORDON: Why I'm here.

SHARON: What?

GORDON: It's very . . . seductive.

SHARON: Good. I want it to be.

SHARON snuggles in.

GORDON: Wait, wait. Sharon. This can't work.

SHARON: It seems to *be* working.

GORDON: I mean. I can't do this with you.

SHARON releases GORDON.

SHARON: I see—

GORDON: —Listen to me, Sharon—

SHARON: —You don't have to explain—

GORDON: This is going to sound, weird, *me* saying this, of all people, but listen. Please. You can do better than this, you *deserve* better than this. You have more dignity than to punish Russel for messing around by sleeping with me—

SHARON grabs GORDON and kisses him again. GORDON retreats.
SHARON slaps him.

SHARON: What do I care about your reflections on my dignity? This is humiliating, this, *this* moment is humiliating. If you don't want to . . . if you don't feel you can . . . Fine.

          But please, don't *advise* me.

GORDON: *(as though still appreciating the lingering sensation of the slap)* Ow.

          Sharon, listen. I know something. Four years ago, Russel was seeing someone else—

SHARON: —Oh please—

GORDON: —Her name was Sheila—

SHARON: —I haven't kept a complete list—

GORDON: —Sheila Beggs, the costume mistress—

SHARON: —I don't want to hear all this—

GORDON: —She's dead now. Did you know that?

Pause.

GORDON: Did you know that, Sharon?

SHARON: No.

GORDON: Do you know who I'm talking about?

SHARON: Yes. I, ah, remember something about her being missing, for a period of time. But what's this got to do with—

GORDON: —Do you remember, shortly before she went missing, Russel doing anything, saying anything—

SHARON: Four years is a long time and what exactly are you saying?

GORDON: I know what happened. Four years ago they went up there, back where I was today. They had a picnic, late at night.

Directly above the house. They could see right down onto the rooftop. She tried to force him to choose. Between you and her. They argued. And in the middle of the argument, he killed her.

Pause.

SHARON: How?

GORDON: He bashed her head in.

SHARON: But how do you know?

GORDON: This is going to sound crazy. But I found something out the other week. When I died.

SHARON: You found something out?

GORDON: I met her.

SHARON: Are you joking?

GORDON: No.

SHARON: You *met* her?

Enter RUSSEL.

RUSSEL: Well, she's going to have the world's largest headache tomorrow. But . . . let's not let the food go to waste, right?

No response.

RUSSEL: What's up?

Still no response.

RUSSEL: What?

SHARON: Gordon has a, notion, that you know what happened to Sheila Beggs.

RUSSEL: Who?

RUSSEL carves himself a piece of the lamb.

GORDON: Look. I know what happened. I know where you tossed her body.

RUSSEL: What's going on? What kind of joke is this?

GORDON: All I want you to do is write out a confession.

RUSSEL: A confession for what? What did you tell him?

SHARON: I didn't tell him anything, Russel. What's this all about?

RUSSEL: You're sitting around here concocting some sort of rubbish—

GORDON: —You hit her head against the rock, you packed her body in an orange garbage bag, you draped her with lead shot weights and you dropped her out there, in the bay, just round the point so the current would take her out rather than back into harbor if she floated up.

Pause.

RUSSEL: How did you know that? It was an *accident.* I was drunk. Things got out of hand.

SHARON: Oh my God.

RUSSEL: When I realized, what had happened . . . what could I *change?* It was done.

SHARON: Oh my God.

RUSSEL: I mean . . . whose interests would it serve to have me in prison? You feel bad, but you fix what you can and you move on. Exactly like everyone else. It was an *accident.* I got carried away.

SHARON: What's happened to you?

RUSSEL: Make me an offer, Gord. What do you want?

GORDON: Nothing.

RUSSEL: I could do something useful, anonymously donate money to the family, to relatives.

GORDON: It's just money.

RUSSEL: Never say it's just money. Money can do an awful lot. Money can do almost anything. What are you doing?

GORDON picks up the phone and dials.

GORDON: Hello. Yes, the police . . . I want to report—

RUSSEL slams the phone down.

RUSSEL: OK. Let's not get silly here.

SHARON: Russel, please. Please, *please* tell me what's going on.

RUSSEL: Gordon, I don't know where you got this information from but it's not the way—

SHARON: —I have put up with so much from you for so long, now what have you gone and—

She grabs RUSSEL.

RUSSEL: —Let go of me—

SHARON: —done. After so many years of *lying* I deserve to know the truth—

RUSSEL: —Let go of me. Let go!

RUSSEL grabs SHARON and propels her backward. She thumps heavily against the wall, sways a moment . . .

SHARON: Ow.

. . . then slides to the floor. Pause.

GORDON: Now, *that* looks remarkably familiar. You standing. Someone of the opposite gender lying on the ground.

RUSSEL: Tell me what you want.

GORDON: You to give yourself up.

RUSSEL: Why your sudden interest in Sheila?

GORDON: You mean, apart from her being dead?

RUSSEL: If I could change history I would—

GORDON: —You already *have*. History is what the living agree upon, and by sinking her body, by removing her name from your date book—

RUSSEL: —*You* took that. That's what you've been doing since you got here, going through my things—

GORDON: —Just by walking about freely now, you rewrite history every day. All I want is that the private history I know becomes the public history we all know.

The phone rings.

GORDON: That'll be the police. They always phone back if a 911 call is interrupted.

GORDON lifts the receiver.

GORDON: Yes, I want to report a murder—

RUSSEL plucks the phone line from its jack in the wall.

RUSSEL: It's just not as satisfying doing that since they installed phone jacks. In the old movies, it always had a certain *je ne sais quois*.

GORDON: They'll come to investigate that interrupted call now.

RUSSEL: You should have gone into the film business, Gord, podiatry has soured you on life. I can see that you're not going to be reasonable. So, I guess I'll have to leave. Which, all things considered, is fine with me. I could use a change. I'll let you take care of Sharon. I'm sure she'll appreciate that, my feeling is she's always secretly preferred you over me anyway.

GORDON: I can't let you go.

RUSSEL: No choice, buddy.

GORDON moves toward RUSSEL.

RUSSEL: I wouldn't do anything stupid now, Gordon. You've never been stupid in the past. Because I am *going* to go. So, stay away from me.

GORDON: Have a seat. Wait for the police to arrive. Explain to them how you accidentally dragged a hundred and twenty pounds over two hundred yards of rough ground and accidentally lost it off the back of your boat.

RUSSEL: Stay back. I'm telling you. I'm telling you.

RUSSEL backs up to the table as GORDON advances on him.

RUSSEL: Stay back.

GORDON comes close enough to take RUSSEL by the shoulders when suddenly GORDON sags. RUSSEL has stabbed him in the belly with the carving knife.

RUSSEL: I *said* stay away from me. That's what comes from not listening.

GORDON collapses to the floor.

RUSSEL: So, car keys, car keys . . . where have I put them . . .

RUSSEL approaches the door to the hallway. It slams shut. RUSSEL tries to open it, but it won't budge.

RUSSEL: What the hell?

RUSSEL pulls on the door. No good. He turns toward the balcony doors. They slam shut. He tries to open them. They won't budge.

RUSSEL: What the hell is going on?

GORDON: You never pay attention to me.

RUSSEL turns and looks at GORDON who is still lying on the floor. Slowly GORDON begins to rise.

GORDON: Remember me saying that?

RUSSEL: What are you talking about?

GORDON: Didn't you hear what I said? "You never pay attention to me." You. Never. Pay. Attention. To me. That's what I said to you the night you killed me, or have you forgotten? Or perhaps it's simply a matter of, once again, not paying attention. To me. Me. Me, Russel, me.

GORDON plucks the knife out and tosses it to the floor.

GORDON: *Sheila.*

RUSSEL: How do you know what Sheila said?

GORDON: You don't get it yet, do you? *I was there.* It's not the sort of thing I'd be likely to forget, is it?

GORDON approaches RUSSEL. He's bleeding from the belly.

GORDON: The way I asked you to make a commitment, the way I begged you to divorce your wife, the way you "accidentally" knocked my head against that rock. That's not the sort of thing that would slip anybody's mind.

RUSSEL tries the door again. It won't open.

GORDON: Since I've been here I've done everything I could to gather evidence. But wherever I went, you'd been there first, sweeping up, dusting up, cleaning up, *expunging.* You've systematically removed, burnt, hidden, sunk every shred, every scrap, every portion of hard, conclusive evidence there is.

RUSSEL: This can't be happening. What the hell is going on?

GORDON: You've just been too clever, Russel. Only now, it's time to give yourself up.

RUSSEL grabs the knife from the floor and stabs GORDON again, twice, then pushes him down. RUSSEL stands, breathing heavily, and then turns toward the balcony again . . . looking for a way out. Suddenly the curtain framing the balcony billows in, even though the doors are shut.

GORDON: I'm still here.

RUSSEL looks down at Gordon's body. The dishes suddenly erupt off the table. GORDON begins to rise again.

GORDON: The problem, Russel, with trying to kill Gordon is . . . Gordon's already dead. I'm just here as a kind of, tenant. See, after he tasted those almonds and went into total arrest, he *did* see the light and he *did* go down that long corridor . . . but, and here I have to admit I haven't been entirely truthful . . . when he went down that long corridor, I was there already. Just off of the corridor, in the waiting room, if you will. Waiting. Waiting. Waiting for *my* chance. And when Gordon looked back at his body, and then at the white light . . . he chose the white light. That, Russel, was my chance. Since he didn't have any more need of his body, I asked if *I* might borrow it. Reduce, re-use, recycle, motto of the responsibly-minded. Right? The only, injunction, he laid on me—out of regard for your friendship—was that I not harm you. And I have . . . gone out of my way not to harm you. Wouldn't you say? Russel?

RUSSEL: Sheila?

GORDON: At last. Recognition.

GORDON thrusts his hands out in front of him and a chair slides back into them.

GORDON: Truthfully, I've been sidetracked in my efforts. It's been much more pleasant than I had anticipated, living again, breathing again, walking on the earth. It's a terrible feeling when all of that is ripped away from you, without warning, let me tell you. When I climbed up the hill this afternoon, it was *so* . . . beautiful, I almost didn't come back. It was that tempting.

RUSSEL: —I didn't mean to do it, Sheila—

GORDON: —Except, now look what you've done. After making it so very difficult for me, you've suddenly made it very easy. All I have to do now is give up this body.

GORDON sets a chair out for RUSSEL to sit on. GORDON raises his arms again and another chair comes rattling to him.

GORDON: *I* know you can't kill me. I'm already dead. But that's not what the police will see when they come here. They'll find this dead body, and your wife knocked unconscious. And you. And your fingerprints all over the murder weapon. And you know the way the police are, they'll just *assume* certain things. So, if they can't convict you for the first murder, they'll certainly convict you for the second.

RUSSEL: I just got, carried away. I, didn't know what to do after—

GORDON: Shh. Not another word.

RUSSEL: I got carried away, Sheila, please, listen—

GORDON: I said shhh!

GORDON gestures and RUSSEL is suddenly unable to speak. The sounds of police sirens.

GORDON: Here they come. Sit down. Rest.

RUSSEL is forced to sit.

GORDON: How long do you think you'll be in prison? How long do you think you'll live to sit and brood and regret all of this? A long time? Maybe even a very long time? Maybe long enough that eventually you'll feel the need to confess to the first murder. Maybe?

A knocking at the door.

GORDON: That's them knocking at the door. I'll leave now, Russel. I'm sorry we couldn't complete the game, but, let's see what the real definition is: Thanatos. Well, what do you know? "Death Personified." Talk about your synchronicity. Thanks for all your co-operation on this matter. And the dinner. It was *excellent.*

More knocking.

GORDON: It's the last time you'll hear from me.

GORDON sinks into a chair, glances about at everything one last time. He draws one deep final breath.

GORDON: Bye bye, Russel.

GORDON exhales. His eyes close and his body relaxes. The sound of the door being kicked in. Fade to black.

End of play.

Monkey Business

By Nicole Zylstra

Monkey Business was commissioned by the Petro-Canada Stage One Plays. It premiered March 8, 2004 at Lunchbox Theatre, Calgary, with the following cast.

HORACE: Ryan Luhning
MYRIAM: Barbara Gates Wilson

Directed by Ian Prinsloo

Set and Lighting Design by Colin Ross

Costumes by Brian Craik

Stage Manager: Marcie Januska

Production Manager: Laura Lee Billing

Technical Director: Peter Cochran

Technician: Cherie Caslyn

Monkey Business was originally workshopped as part of the Petro-Canada Stage One Plays in May of 2003 with Barbara Gates Wilson (Myriam), and Ryan Luhning (Horace). The workshop was directed by Ian Prinsloo. Stage directions were read by Breanne Feigel. Christopher Cinnamon was the Dramaturge Assistant. The technician was Michael Olson. The Production Manager was Laura Lee Billing.

Characters

MYRIAM

HORACE

Setting: A rainforest in Costa Rica. HORACE and MYRIAM are here as part of a university research project to collect data from howler monkeys. They tranquilize them, catch them in nets, and take imprints of their teeth. They also collect fecal matter, and observe what the monkeys eat. The purpose of the project is to collect enough information from these and other primates to cross-reference the dental findings with those of early hominids, in the hope of discovering what early man ate. This has very little to do with the rest of the play . . .

Scene One: Leap

Sound of a small gun, like a starter's pistol. Lights up on HORACE and MYRIAM holding a large net. They peer into the tree canopy above them. They wait.

HORACE:	Leap and the net will appear.
MYRIAM:	What's that?
HORACE:	Sorry. I just thought it was funny. "Leap and the net will appear." And here we are. With a net.
MYRIAM:	Come on, come on, come on.
HORACE:	What's the rush? Gotta be somewhere?
MYRIAM:	We've been waiting for a long time. Where did you hit him?
HORACE:	Does it matter?
MYRIAM:	Yes.
HORACE:	I think in the foot.
MYRIAM:	You did hit him, didn't you?

HORACE: Of course I did. I think. No, I did. I did. He'll come down. Don't worry.

HORACE and MYRIAM wait. And wait. MYRIAM is focused. HORACE is enjoying the scenery. He sees a big bad-ass spider. He looks somewhere else.

HORACE: Why do you think they call them howler monkeys?

Sound of a howler monkey "chattering."

HORACE: Jesus Christ.

MYRIAM: Nope, just a howler.

HORACE: Ignore my earlier question.

MYRIAM sighs.

HORACE: Is that a spider?

MYRIAM: Probably.

HORACE: No kidding. It's big. I was hoping it was just a rat. Do you think it's poisonous?

MYRIAM: Yup.

HORACE steps away.

MYRIAM: Keep the net tight, Horace.

HORACE: Sorry, Myriam. It's kind of hard with just the two of us.

MYRIAM: And whose fault is that?

HORACE: I'm gonna take a wild guess that you are implying it's my fault somehow.

MYRIAM: Who got the other guys so drunk last night that they can't move today?

HORACE: Technically, the dysentery isn't my fault.

MYRIAM: But the dehydration . . . the alcohol poisoning . . .

HORACE: Screw 'em if they can't hold their liquor, that's what I say. Bunch of university guys should have more stamina than that.

MYRIAM doesn't respond.

HORACE: I think you're just steamed because you went to bed early.

MYRIAM: I was exhausted. Yesterday was really hard. And it's not easy being the boss of you guys.

HORACE: Overwhelmed by the sizzling masculine energy?

MYRIAM: Exhausted by the witty banter, more like. Do all guys have to take some sort of course in high school where they make you memorize every episode of the *The Simpsons* and teach you how to make funny sound effects? Or is that some underground ritual?

HORACE: Rite of passage. Goes back to our caveman roots when we had to make funny noises to survive.

MYRIAM: Fantastic. So it's not something you evolve out of?

HORACE: The pop cultural references change, but the song remains the same, I'm afraid. *The Simpsons* are just carrying the torch passed down from Monty Python.

MYRIAM: Ergh. It's no fair. Why should I feel like I have a hangover when I didn't even drink?

HORACE: Serves you right. Next time you'll know better. I promise I'll get you drunk next time.

MYRIAM: If you plan on doing to me whatever you did to those other fellas, you can forget about it. Not that I'm a teetotaler, mind you. I can drink as much as the next guy. I just don't need to kill myself doing it.

HORACE: Hey, I got them started, but it's not my fault they don't know when to stop. As you'll notice, I'm in fine form this morning.

MYRIAM: Actually, that's not true.

HORACE: I'm not in fine form?

MYRIAM: I can't drink as much as the next guy. I am the cheapest drunk in the world.

HORACE: Rrrreally?

MYRIAM stares up into the forest canopy.

MYRIAM: It's true, to my everlasting shame. How I ever made it through my undergraduate degree I'll never know. One beer and I'm tipsy. Two and I'm plastered. Three and I'm under the table . . .

HORACE: Interesting. Now when you say "under the table" what exactly are you doing?

MYRIAM: *(still looking up)* Look out!

HORACE: Whoa!

A sleeping howler monkey falls from the sky into the net.

MYRIAM: Got him.

HORACE: Nice work.

Scene Two: Shot Down

MYRIAM: Pull!

And the sound of the tranquilizer gun. Monkey chattering. Lights up on HORACE and MYRIAM with the net.

HORACE: Why do you say "pull" every time, like you're shooting skeet?

MYRIAM: I don't know. I guess because it reminds me of shooting skeet.

HORACE: But you're not killing pigeons.

MYRIAM: You can't kill clay pigeons.

HORACE: No, but these guys aren't clay.

MYRIAM: No, but we're not killing them either. We're just making them sleepy for a while. Tranquilizing them.

HORACE: Making them tranquil. Is that really what we're doing? Do they look tranquil to you?

MYRIAM: Of course they do. They're asleep.

HORACE: But "asleep" and "tranquil" are not necessarily the same thing.

MYRIAM: Does it matter? Does it have to be exactly the same thing? Asleep, tranquil. Monkeys, pigeons. You don't like to pretend once in a while?

HORACE: I'd rather not get into the whole bedroom thing right away if you don't mind. I thought this was a professional relationship.

MYRIAM: It is.

HORACE: Good. So professionally speaking would you go out with me?

MYRIAM: Watch it!

HORACE: Sorry.

A monkey falls into their net.

MYRIAM: We're making good time.

HORACE: Speak for yourself.

Scene Three: Aim

HORACE takes aim with the tranquilizer gun.

MYRIAM: Careful.

HORACE:	What?
MYRIAM:	He's right over you.
HORACE:	So?
MYRIAM:	So, if he drops a sample, you're right in the line of fire.
HORACE:	It's all right. I'd rather get it in the face than in my hair anyway.
MYRIAM:	I know a lot of gals who say the same thing.

HORACE blanches, shocked.

Scene Four: Fire

HORACE and MYRIAM sit with binoculars, looking for signs that the monkeys have started eating.

HORACE:	Why not?
MYRIAM:	Because you're a grad student and I'm a professor.
HORACE:	You're a post-doc on a two-year contract. You don't even have tenure.
MYRIAM:	Ooh. That's the way to woo a woman. Keep looking, Horace.
HORACE:	I am looking.
MYRIAM:	At the monkeys. We have to record everything they eat.
HORACE:	I know, I know. Once they start eating, I'm all over it. Meanwhile, don't change the subject. Give me a better reason.
MYRIAM:	Well, how about because you're . . . your age, and I'm . . . you know . . . Not.
HORACE:	You're sensitive about your age?

MYRIAM:	Not exactly. Sort of. But I'm old enough to know better than to date someone your age, no offense.
HORACE:	None taken. What's wrong with someone my age?
MYRIAM:	Nothing. It's lovely. You're lovely.
HORACE:	Thank you.
MYRIAM:	You're welcome.
HORACE:	So go out with me.
MYRIAM:	I can't.
HORACE:	Can't or won't?
MYRIAM:	What's the difference?
HORACE:	"Can't" means there is something physically in the way, some real-world obstacle. "Can't" means that we are separated by something—by geography, mortality, a rift in the space-time continuum for instance. Now we know that that's not true. After all, here we are.
MYRIAM:	With this net between us.
HORACE:	Yes. Interesting.
MYRIAM:	Is it?
HORACE:	Very. Does the net separate us? Or does it hold us together?
MYRIAM:	Good question. What's the answer?
HORACE:	There is no answer. The answer is all dependent on your perspective. Remember. Perspective is everything.
MYRIAM:	Sorry. I don't read the *Globe and Mail.*
HORACE:	Not even on Saturdays?
MYRIAM:	OK, I do the crossword. And read my horoscope.
HORACE:	How uncharacteristically unscientific of you.

MYRIAM: Oh, I don't believe in that stuff. I don't think the stars can predict that you and one twelfth of the population will have exactly the same kind of day. I just think the Universe is speaking only to me, personally through the medium of the paper.

HORACE: You think the Universe is sending you messages?

MYRIAM: You think it isn't?

HORACE: Not at all. It probably is.

MYRIAM: Do you read your horoscope?

HORACE: Never. I don't need messages from the Universe to tell me how to conduct my day. I have staggering confidence in my own abilities. Of course I *would* say that; I'm a typical Leo. Now let's get back to my question. "Can't" or "won't." Well, we've eliminated "can't."

MYRIAM: That leaves us with Hegel. Ba-dum, pum-ching.

HORACE: Shhh. So that leaves us with "won't." Hmmm. Now why "won't?" What other internal mechanism is at work here? What act of self-will are you perpetrating by not following your instincts? "Won't" means you refuse because . . . well only you can answer that.

MYRIAM: OK. Let's say I won't because I don't see it as a viable option.

HORACE: I love it when you talk saucy to me. But seriously, I want to get to the bottom of this. Going out with me is not a viable option because . . . well it could be because you don't find me attractive. Fine. I would accept that.

MYRIAM: Good.

HORACE: Do you find me unattractive?

MYRIAM: I didn't say that.

HORACE: So you find me attractive.

MYRIAM: I didn't say that either.

HORACE: So you refuse to answer the question?

MYRIAM: Yes.

HORACE: Because you're afraid to admit you're attracted to me.

MYRIAM: Why would I be afraid of that?

HORACE: You tell me.

MYRIAM: I'm not afraid.

HORACE: So you are attracted to me.

MYRIAM: What?

HORACE: And why wouldn't you be?

MYRIAM: You're pretty sure of yourself.

HORACE: I'm telling it like it is.

MYRIAM: Do you get a lot of dates using Socratic Method?

HORACE: Hundreds. I find it works better than Sarcastic Method. Now where were we? You've already admitted you're attracted to me. So why don't we say eight o'clock, my tent? I'll make dinner. Which do you prefer? The white or the red can?

MYRIAM: You move fast, don't you?

HORACE: I don't believe in wasting time.

MYRIAM: Funny you should put it that way. Because if I agreed to go out with you, isn't that what it would be?

HORACE: A waste of time?

MYRIAM: Yes.

HORACE: Why?

MYRIAM: Because . . . because of the objections I've already raised.

HORACE: I don't see those as viable objections, to use your terminology.

MYRIAM: Look. I'm not saying that it wouldn't be a good time. But I've had a lot of good times in my life, and quite frankly, a good time is just not what I'm looking for these days.

HORACE: I can arrange for us to have a really bad time, if you want.

MYRIAM: How thoughtful. No. It's this: I don't need a good time as much as I need someone to enjoy the bad times with. If that makes any sense.

HORACE: OK, I get it. You don't want to get hurt.

MYRIAM: Who does? Do you?

HORACE: Of course not.

MYRIAM: Well, then . . .

HORACE: Well then what?

MYRIAM: Well, then, let's Not and say We Did, or whatever. Let's just enjoy each other's company without . . .

HORACE: Without risking it.

MYRIAM: Exactly.

HORACE: Life is about risk.

MYRIAM: No. You don't understand. Why would we—

HORACE: Why would we start something when we can already see the ending?

MYRIAM: Exactly.

Monkey drops.

Scene Five: Breathe

HORACE and MYRIAM try various yoga poses to try and hold the net taut.

HORACE: Are you sure this is safe?

MYRIAM: Sure. I learned this in yoga class.

HORACE: You were saying?

MYRIAM: I was saying, it flies counter to everything, instinctually.

HORACE: In what way?

MYRIAM: Well, the point of every species—the point of Life—is survival. And so the only way to survive as a species is to reproduce. You aren't going to live forever, and so you have to make your contribution as a species. You reproduce. And die. And the next generation lives on.

HORACE: Perfecting itself.

MYRIAM: Well, not exactly. But continuing, certainly. The point of Life is Reproduction. Once you've reproduced, you've pretty much blown your wad, and decline into death.

HORACE: Well that's a romantic view of it.

MYRIAM: I'm thinking botany, now. Plants whose "fair flow'r, being once displayed, doth fall that very hour." The flower comes to fruition and the fair blossom is blown once she has opened herself and given her precious pollen to the bees.

HORACE: Well, it doesn't happen exactly like that. But it's a beautiful image. Like poetry.

MYRIAM: It is. Shakespeare. Of course he was talking about women.

HORACE: Really?

MYRIAM: Yes. In *Twelfth Night*, Count Orsino says to Viola, who is disguised as a boy and is in love with him; "Then let thy love be younger than thyself, For women are as roses, whose fair flow'r, once displayed, doth fall that very hour." She says to him, "And so they are; alas, that they are so. To die, even when they to perfection grow."

HORACE: Beautiful. But a total crock.

MYRIAM: How so?

HORACE: The point of Life is Death.

MYRIAM: Well that's a bit morbid, isn't it?

HORACE: No, it's just as fact.

MYRIAM: I think death is a by-product of successful reproduction. Nature has done her job in producing, and so the producer is done for.

HORACE: With an attitude like that I'm not surprised you don't have kids.

MYRIAM: Ouch. Point of the knife taken. Straight to the heart.

HORACE: Sorry. I didn't mean it like that.

MYRIAM: It's all right. You're probably right. And so I would still say to you, "let thy love be younger than thyself, or thy affection cannot hold the bent."

HORACE: OK, you have to stop with the Shakespeare. I can't compete with that.

MYRIAM: Sorry. I took a lot of English classes as an undergrad.

HORACE: But if the point is that you think you're a . . . fading flower who is outliving her usefulness as a member of the species . . . Wow. If that's what you think, well, you're pretty hard on yourself.

MYRIAM: Yes. I'm brutal. Brutally honest.

HORACE: No. Just brutal. The point of Life is Death. Point A: Birth. Point B: Death. A straight line. Well. Maybe more interesting than that. Between points A and B there is an infinite amount of possibility. Isn't it in our own interest to explore as much of that as we can? Why limit yourself to biological imperative?

A monkey falls in the net.

Scene Six: Scat

HORACE and MYRIAM are up with the net again.

HORACE: Chairman Meow.

MYRIAM: Good one.

HORACE: What's your cat's name?

MYRIAM: Apollo.

HORACE: Greek mythology?

MYRIAM: *Battlestar Galactica*. But he has about a million nicknames. Starting with Poo. Poo-head. Poodle.

HORACE: Poodle?

MYRIAM: Because it's funny if a cat has a dog's name. Poodle turns into pooch. And then Pooch turns into its own series of nicknames. Pooch. Poochkin. Alexander Poochkin. Giacomo Poochini. Etc. etc.

HORACE: You have a lot of time on your hands.

MYRIAM: I have a lot of time at home with my cat. I know someone that named their cat "Raoul."

HORACE: Nice.

MYRIAM: That way the cat always knew his own name.

HORACE: What?

MYRIAM: *(she meows)* "Raoul."

HORACE: Very nice. I play head games with my cat.

MYRIAM: How?

HORACE: He'll come up to me looking all serious and sober and meow at me and I just look at him and say, "Speak ENGLISH, I don't UNDERSTAND you!"

MYRIAM: And does he?

HORACE: No, he just looks at me more intently and meows again. But I know he's thinking, "You're such an idiot. Speak CAT, I don't UNDERSTAND you."

MYRIAM: Actually, cats only meow at people. They don't meow at other cats. So technically he's saying "You're such an idiot. I AM speaking English." Ha. It's so great to talk to someone who likes cats. It seems like everyone's allergic these days. That's one of my pet peeves—people whose throats close up when they enter a room where a cat might have passed through ten years ago. Erh! It drives me up the wall. I know technically they can't help it but I swear they do it on purpose. I hate them.

HORACE: Me too! See, we have so much in common.

MYRIAM: It's a coincidence.

HORACE: It's fate.

MYRIAM: Fate is for sissies.

HORACE: Really?

MYRIAM: Yup. I'd rather take my own fate in my own hands thank you very much, and chew on the consequences later.

HORACE: So you believe in self-determination?

MYRIAM: Sure. Don't you?

HORACE: I believe in evolution.

MYRIAM: I didn't think the two were mutually exclusive.

HORACE: Self-determination is arrogant. It puts you at the centre of your universe, making the world subservient to your will.

MYRIAM: Yes. I told you, I do that.

HORACE: And evolution is fate. Fate puts the world's will above your own. Much more relaxing to yield to the will of the world, don't you think?

MYRIAM: Evolution is not fate. Evolution is random.

HORACE: But it is also fate: things evolve a certain way because they were always meant to do so. If they weren't, they would have turned out some other way.

MYRIAM: From the book, "Blue is the Color of the Sky Because the Sky is Blue . . . and Other Great Tautologies to Live By."

HORACE: Ooh. Good use of the word "tautology." How long have you been waiting to use that one in a sentence?

MYRIAM: About five years. But that's not the point.

HORACE: The point is exactly that.

MYRIAM: What?

HORACE: That there is no point.

MYRIAM: Now you're just talking to hear yourself speak.

HORACE: Yes, but I do have a point.

MYRIAM: I thought the point was that there is no point.

HORACE: Exactly my point.

A monkey falls into the net. MYRIAM picks him up and carefully, while HORACE rolls up the net.

HORACE: Close call. That makes seven. Almost through?

MYRIAM: There's about twelve in this colony. More than half-way.

HORACE: Excellent. Shall we take some dental imprints while this little fella's still asleep and then resume our philosophical debate later? Over a thermos of Scotch perhaps?

MYRIAM: You start with the dental molds. I'm going to collect scat samples.

HORACE: I'm gonna send the university my own scat sample.

MYRIAM: Horace.

HORACE: No no no. Like this, "scooby do wah scat cha chaaaa."

MYRIAM: All right, Ella. Bring it down a notch.

HORACE: Fine. Shit-disturber.

Scene Seven: What do you Meme by That?

MYRIAM: Flip-flops. "It's a Small World After All." Capri pants. Goth. Quoting *The Simpsons*. How to build an arch. The belief in Life After Death. How to make fire. The "Cheap Sperm/Expensive Egg" theory of sexual behavior. Uh, "Peace out." "Bling-bling." Tap dancing. Any symbol that has stood the test of time: the Silver Moon, the Golden Sun, Mother Earth.

HORACE: OK, I think I get it. Like uh, The Good Guy Wears a White Hat, or the hula hoop, or electricity for that matter. Quantum physics. "What's Up Doc?" "You dirty rat." The space-time continuum. Shoelaces and how to tie them. Playing "Time of Your Life" under Powerpoint presentations and slideshows. These are all cultural memes, right?

MYRIAM: Right. Because they're ideas that leap from brain to brain, breeding themselves spontaneously. Like a virus forces us to spread it through a sneeze. We sneeze these ideas from our brains to others, and—

HORACE: And they tell two friends, and then they tell two friends, and so on, and so on, and so on.

MYRIAM: Oooh . . . I love it! You just used a meme on itself, to describe itself, it's like a snake eating its own tail. Which is another meme.

HORACE: I can't believe it—this is actually turning you on, isn't it.

MYRIAM: A little bit.

HORACE: Cool. Which reminds me: two chicks getting it on. That's another meme specific to heterosexual males.

MYRIAM: Totally. See, there's even a theory that personality is nothing but a series of acquired memes. So you —the idea of "you," your ego in fact—might be nothing more than the collection of ideas that have rubbed up against you over time.

HORACE: You're saying I've been raped by ideas and they become who I am?

MYRIAM: Why do you say raped? Do you feel violated by the ideas that make you up? I may have been pushed up against the wall by Shakespeare in the same way that you have been rolled by *The Simpsons*, but I loved every minute of it.

HORACE: You cultural whore.

MYRIAM: I am. I'll make wild passionate monkey-love to any new idea that brushes against me. It may only be a fling, and I may push that idea out the door in the morning, but We'll Always Have Paris. Which is another meme.

HORACE: I get it.

MYRIAM: I know, but it was kind of a joke.

HORACE: Kind of.

Playful swatting ensues. Monkey falls—they catch it in the nick of time.

Scene Eight: Spoon Worm

MYRIAM: The Green Spoon Worm.

HORACE: No kidding.

MYRIAM: Yup. The males are 200,000 times smaller than the female. She basically inhales him and he makes his way down to her reproductive tract where he fertilizes passing eggs. He sets up house in a place in her body called an "androecium," or literally, "small man room."

HORACE: Sounds like a relationship I had once.

MYRIAM: No kidding.

HORACE: No. No kidding.

Long pause.

MYRIAM: You've been quiet.

HORACE: Have I? Sorry. Nothing personal.

MYRIAM: We're getting through them pretty quickly. The monkeys, I mean.

HORACE: Yeah.

MYRIAM: You had good aim on the last one. This one shouldn't take long.

Pause

MYRIAM: You bored?

HORACE: What? Oh. No.

Pause.

MYRIAM: Horace.

HORACE: Hmm?

MYRIAM: What is it?

HORACE: Nothing to tell.

MYRIAM: Nah, c'mon, everybody's got something.

HORACE: Sorry. What you see is what you get. I'm an open book.

MYRIAM: Yeah. But there's a lot of small print under the pretty pictures. C'mon. Spit it out.

HORACE: I don't know what you're getting at.

MYRIAM: Are we going to have to do this the hard way?

HORACE: Looks like it.

MYRIAM: Let's look at the facts first.

HORACE: Always a good idea.

MYRIAM: What do we know about you? Well, you're charming, intelligent, witty.

HORACE: Thank you, thank you, and thank you.

MYRIAM: What's your background?

HORACE: Nothing special.

MYRIAM: How did you get this job? What's your area of study?

HORACE: Human nature.

MYRIAM: I'm betting you're a Political Science major, slumming in Anthro to fill out your character a bit.

HORACE: Nope.

MYRIAM: OK. Well, you make too much sense to actually be studying Philosophy. So my next guess is . . . Humanistic Studies. That would be a nice vague major which would allow you to indulge your obviously eclectic tastes, and would also make your comment about studying "human nature" one of your typically witty twists on the truth. Ha? Am I right?

HORACE: Way off.

MYRIAM: You're not actually in Anthropology are you? Oh wait—I bet you're one of those sneaky Cultural Anthro types. Those guys think everything is relative. That would fit with your casual laid-back attitude and disdain for empirical truth. That's it, isn't it?

HORACE: Not even close.

MYRIAM: You've got to be kidding. OK, what is it, then? What's your major?

HORACE: I don't have one.

MYRIAM: General Studies. I knew it. Hey—that's cheating—I said Humanistic Studies and that's the same thing.

HORACE: No, I mean I don't have one. I don't have a major because I'm not enrolled in the university.

MYRIAM: What? That's not possible. How did you get on this job? It's only open to students.

HORACE: And staff.

MYRIAM: Staff? You teach?

HORACE: I look after the gardens.

MYRIAM: Botany?

HORACE: I'm in landscaping.

MYRIAM: Landscaping?

HORACE: I mow the lawn. Well, and other things. I water the lawn too.

MYRIAM: Really? Trim the hedges and all that? Plant the annuals? Prune the perennials?

HORACE: Anything wrong with that?

MYRIAM: No. I think it's fascinating.

HORACE: You trying to study me, now?

MYRIAM: A little bit.

HORACE: It's a boring subject.

MYRIAM: Defensive?

HORACE: No. Of course not.

MYRIAM: Then let me ask you a question.

HORACE: OK.

MYRIAM: What's on your bookshelf?

HORACE: I don't have one.

MYRIAM: Don't be ridiculous, of course you have one.

HORACE: I don't.

MYRIAM: Then where do you keep your books?

HORACE: I don't have any.

MYRIAM: If you don't read, how do you know so much about, you know, everything.

HORACE: I didn't say I didn't read. I said I don't have a bookshelf. I have a book on the back of my toilet. I read it, and then I get rid of it and get a new one.

MYRIAM: So the back of your toilet is your bookshelf.

HORACE: I suppose.

MYRIAM: That tells me a lot.

HORACE: Like what?

MYRIAM: First, I'm not sure I believe you.

HORACE: You think I'd lie?

MYRIAM: I think you'd continue to bait me if it proved profitable. But let's assume you're telling the truth and the bathroom is your library. What's the last book you read?

HORACE: Something by John Ralston Saul.

MYRIAM: And before that?

HORACE: I re-read *Batman: the Dark Knight*.

MYRIAM: The graphic novel?

HORACE: You know it?

MYRIAM: Of course I do. It's a classic. So you read philosophy and comic books. See, it just doesn't add up.

HORACE: Too weird?

MYRIAM: No. It's too perfect. Like you're trying to prove something.

HORACE: Like what?

MYRIAM: That's what I'm trying to figure out. Unless you just want to tell me.

HORACE: Look, Myriam, I'm a little tired right now.

MYRIAM: Is something wrong?

HORACE: No.

MYRIAM: Did I say something?

HORACE: No.

MYRIAM: Anything you want to talk about?

HORACE: Just drop it. Nothing personal.

Scene Nine: Artichoke & Flower

MYRIAM and HORACE sit with their net between them.

MYRIAM: Why me?

HORACE: Why not you?

MYRIAM: Not good enough.

HORACE:	I don't know then.
MYRIAM:	Worse.
HORACE:	Why don't I ask you then. Why not me?
MYRIAM:	There are a million reasons. Or at least tens of thousands spanning the years of human evolution.
HORACE:	Let's make it easy on ourselves and start at the beginning. Number one. Go.
MYRIAM:	You're too young.
HORACE:	How so? I'm way over eighteen. I can show you my drivers' license if you want.
MYRIAM:	I know you're over eighteen.
HORACE:	So I'm past the first flush of youth.
MYRIAM:	Rapidly passing your sexual prime, some would say.
HORACE:	While you are approaching yours. Sounds like a good blend to me.
MYRIAM:	And yet you are still under thirty.
HORACE:	A goodly age, as they say. Ripe for the picking. Past the age of dalliance and approaching wisdom.
MYRIAM:	The truly wise know they know nothing. And so you are yet too young for me.
HORACE:	Do you think you're wise?
MYRIAM:	No. Not at all. But I know enough to know I know nothing.
HORACE:	If you know nothing, how do you know I'm too young for you? Perhaps I'm just right.
MYRIAM:	And what if you were? What am I to you then?
HORACE:	A woman. What are you worried about?

MYRIAM: Let's say I let you catch me in your net. And it's all hunky-dory—for a while. And then one day you might sit back and look at me for the first time. Then you would see exactly how old I am. And one day it will catch up with me. And while age makes men look distinguished, it makes women look . . . tired. You will continue to ripen with age, my beautiful young friend. And lines will only add to your charm, and silver hair will only add to your perceived wisdom. And women younger than you, by more years than separate you and I—sparkling, rapturous, fertile women—will seek you out. What is to stop you then from obeying an impulse as natural to man as evolution is to nature?

HORACE: A pretty speech. But a crock. Who's to say what will happen? Maybe you'll get hit by a bus.

MYRIAM: Cheery thought.

HORACE: Or me? Who's to say either of us will live that long? Time is friend to neither of us.

MYRIAM: OK. But the odds are—

HORACE: The odds are that you aren't aware of all the possibilities. Are you aware of my heart condition?

MYRIAM: What?

HORACE: It runs in the family. All the men in my father's family in documented history have all died before the age of forty.

MYRIAM: Oh my God.

HORACE: Talk about odds. I've lived with that all my life. The point is, would that change your mind at all? About our respective ages? Are you looking forward, or looking back, is what I'm asking. Where does the time thing catch up to you? Is it that I have two few years behind me, or ahead of me?

MYRIAM: Gosh, I don't know. I'm sorry, I had no idea. Really. Is it safe for you to be here? Honestly, I had no idea. And I made you push the van out of the ditch!

HORACE: It's OK. Really.

MYRIAM: No, it's not. You should tell people.

HORACE: Why?

MYRIAM: Because.

HORACE: Because why? So it would change their perception of me? I don't think so.

MYRIAM: But on a practical level. We have to know things like that on a job like this. It's important. Are you OK now? Do you need to lie down?

HORACE: Why Doctor, that's the best offer I've had all day.

MYRIAM: Cut it out, Horace. Are you really all right?

HORACE: Honestly Myriam, it is beside the point.

MYRIAM: No it isn't. Now you have me all worried.

HORACE: Don't worry.

MYRIAM: Why not?

HORACE: Because I'll be fine.

MYRIAM: How do you know? You just said you can't know anything.

HORACE: Yes, I did.

MYRIAM: So how can you know? And especially considering . . . Why didn't anyone tell me? Didn't you have to have a medical or something before coming down here?

HORACE: No.

MYRIAM: You didn't?

HORACE: Yes. I did. But it was fine.

MYRIAM: How could that be?

HORACE: Well. I may have been slightly bullshitting.

MYRIAM: What do you mean? You lied on your medical report?

HORACE: I don't have a heart condition.

MYRIAM: What?

HORACE: I'm healthy as a horse.

MYRIAM: Horace! What are you trying to do to me?

HORACE: It's nice to know you care.

MYRIAM: Of course I care. God. Of course. A monkey would care. I'm not completely insensitive. I'm not heartless. You bastard!

HORACE: Uh-oh.

MYRIAM: How could you lie about something like that?

HORACE: I was trying to prove a point.

MYRIAM: You are a vicious liar.

HORACE: Not necessarily – !

MYRIAM: Stop! Just stop whatever's going to roll off that forked tongue of yours.

HORACE: Now hear me out.

MYRIAM: Why should I? You just convinced me you had a heart condition. Why should I listen to anything you say. God, I'm gullible.

HORACE: I know. That's one of the things I like about you. Your innate faith in human nature.

MYRIAM: Well, it's gone. I won't believe a thing you say from here on in.

HORACE: Oh don't be that way.

MYRIAM: What way?

HORACE: All insulted. It's just going to get in the way.

MYRIAM: How should I be? You lied to me, you bastard. About something important.

HORACE: But I didn't really.

MYRIAM: So now you have a heart condition? Are you just going to keep changing your story until you get what you want out of me?

HORACE: Yes. Kidding. No. Of course not. Now listen. OK, maybe I don't have a heart condition. Right now. But I could.

MYRIAM: How are you winning your argument this way?

HORACE: I'm serious. The men on my father's side are extremely short-lived, and all the men on my mother's side of the family live to be a hundred. Now where does that leave me? Living in uncertainty. Which is where we all are. Isn't it? The point is we don't know what time is available to us, so we have to make the time worthwhile while we have it.

MYRIAM: You can't just keep twisting things whichever way you–

HORACE: Hear me out. Who is to say you won't tire of me first? If you've got a bad-ass case of commitaphobia, which is what I would diagnose if I had my druthers–

MYRIAM: Which you don't–

HORACE: Nonetheless. If you are indeed a classic commitaphobe then I have more to worry about than you do. Are you?

MYRIAM: A classic commitaphobe?

HORACE: Yes.

MYRIAM: Maybe.

HORACE: Example.

MYRIAM: I lived with a man for five years and always kept our books and CDs scrupulously separate. I would get highly annoyed if I found one of my books on his shelf.

HORACE: Why?

MYRIAM: People might think it was a clue to his personality instead of a marker defining mine.

HORACE: Wow. That's pretty bad.

MYRIAM: I know.

HORACE: So books are the key to your personality?

MYRIAM: One of them. I think I keep them around like little genetic markers. You can read a double helix and learn a lot about a person, but you can read a bookshelf and learn a lot more about a personality.

HORACE: So you're a snob.

MYRIAM: No. I don't necessarily care what's ON your bookshelf, as long as something's there. I just think that a person who doesn't read anything at all must have no curiosity about the world, and such a person doesn't deserve to be a part of it.

HORACE: A part of what?

MYRIAM: The world.

HORACE: So you are a snob.

MYRIAM: I am not a snob.

HORACE: OK, you're an elitist.

MYRIAM: Maybe. I don't know. Maybe I'm a snob.

HORACE: No you're not.

MYRIAM: You just said I was.

HORACE: I was just baiting you.

MYRIAM: Just to see what I'd say?

HORACE: Yup.

MYRIAM: Do you do that a lot?

HORACE: Yes.

MYRIAM: You are maddening! And I really shouldn't take you seriously at all.

HORACE: On the contrary, take me very seriously. I am your divining rod. You will learn a lot about yourself by just bouncing that over-busy brain of yours against my serene wall of accusations.

MYRIAM: What makes you think my brain is over-busy?

HORACE: Three things. Your propensity for quoting Shakespeare in the jungle. Your use of "tautology" in a sentence. And the fact that you worry about what it might say about you if someone slipped a book that wasn't yours onto your shelf. That, I'm presuming, is worse than finding one of your books on someone else's shelf?

MYRIAM: Absolutely. Oh God, yes.

HORACE: I have half a mind to slip into your house one day and replace every other book with Oprah's Book Club picks.

MYRIAM: What makes you think that I would find that offensive?

HORACE: You're a snob.

MYRIAM: My God you're right. I would HATE that.

HORACE: Don't worry about it. It's all right.

MYRIAM: Why is it all right? It's downright rude. That's what I am.

HORACE: Honestly. It's a small thing. I forgive you.

MYRIAM: Why?

HORACE: Because it's ultimately pointless. You can't define a person by their books any more than you can define someone by their medical records. It's just a quirk you have. Quirks are endearing.

MYRIAM: Don't say that.

HORACE: Why not?

MYRIAM: Because I hate quirks.

HORACE: What do you mean?

MYRIAM: I hate especially quirky females.

HORACE: Why on earth is that?

MYRIAM: Because it's an overused stereotype that I despise. On television, in the movies, it's a meme gone mad. There's the quirky girl and the uptight guy and he doesn't know how to enjoy life and she puts maple syrup on toast and has a weird collection of hats or something and they both Learn A Lot About Life from each other. Blech. I loathe it.

HORACE: Loathe is a strong word.

MYRIAM: That's why I used it.

HORACE: Why do you hate these stories so much?

MYRIAM: Because it reduces women into easily pigeonholed caricatures. I am not a caricature. I'm more complex than that.

HORACE: So am I.

MYRIAM: No one said you weren't.

HORACE: You did.

MYRIAM: When?

HORACE: All day. You've reduced me to a classic meme: the Callow Youth. Is that fair?

MYRIAM: Perhaps not.

HORACE: After all, I have quirks too.

MYRIAM: Apparently. Like toying with people's delicate faith in human nature like a cat plays with a twist tie.

HORACE: No, no, no. Something more mundane.

MYRIAM: Like what, Mr. Machiavelli?

HORACE: I have a collection of weird hats.

MYRIAM: You do not.

HORACE: OK, OK. But I play the ukulele.

MYRIAM: Why?

HORACE: When I was a kid I wanted to learn the guitar but my parents couldn't afford to buy me one, but they found this perfectly good ukulele at a garage sale. So I had to learn to play it. Taught myself too. But I hated the sheet music they put out for the ukulele. I wanted to play guitar, remember. So I just played the music I liked.

MYRIAM: Which was?

HORACE: Mostly heavy metal bands.

MYRIAM: Wow. That's good. That's weird.

HORACE: I know. I'll play you something next time you're at my apartment.

MYRIAM: Nice try.

HORACE: I'll win you over yet. You see, you just never know about people. You make judgments too quickly.

MYRIAM: Perhaps I do.

HORACE: It's all right, it's one of your quirks. What's another one?

MYRIAM: I don't have any.

HORACE: Liar. Do you have a weird collection of hats?

MYRIAM: No. No, no no.

HORACE: But you have . . .

MYRIAM: What?

HORACE: You tell me.

MYRIAM: Nothing.

HORACE: You have a collection of hands.

MYRIAM: What?

HORACE: Ape hands. And human. Skeleton ones. I've seen them in your office at the university.

MYRIAM: So? Who doesn't?

HORACE: A lot of people.

MYRIAM: I'm a paleoanthropologist. I study evolution. It's not surprising or unusual that I have a few casts or specimens in my office.

HORACE: That you use as paperweights?

MYRIAM: Is that quirky?

HORACE: I'm afraid so.

MYRIAM: Damn. Damn damn damn. I'm getting rid of them when I get back.

HORACE: Oh no. Don't do that. But tell me. Why do you have them around?

MYRIAM: They make good paperweights.

HORACE: So do rocks. Why do you use skeleton hands?

MYRIAM: Keeps me in touch with my work, I guess.

HORACE: More than that. There's another reason.

MYRIAM: How do you know?

HORACE: Because you're giving me the logical reasons. There's always an illogical one and that one is the most telling. Think about it.

MYRIAM: I guess they're good reminders.

HORACE: Of what?

MYRIAM: Of mortality. I can have a cast of a hand that belonged to someone 10,000 years ago. And they probably thought they were doing something pretty important with it at the time. And here it is. 10,000 years later. On my desk. And one day maybe my hand will be holding down someone else's papers or holding someone's door open. That's just the way of the world

HORACE: And why hands? Why not skulls? Lots of people collect skulls, it seems to me.

MYRIAM: Skulls are all well and good, but our hands are distinctly ours. *Homo habilis*, the handyman, that's our heritage. We think of great schemes with our big brains, but we build them, we make them reality with our hands. To me that's distinctly human. Dolphins are supposed to be pretty bright too. Maybe smarter than we are, who knows. But a dolphin didn't build the cathedral at Notre Dame. We express our hopes and dreams, from our simplest needs—shelter—to our most complex abstract spiritual aspirations through our hands. After all, what is the cathedral at Notre Dame or the Sistine Chapel if not a way to manifest awe—to stir in us a feeling of the sublime; to make manifest the experience of God.

HORACE: Good answer.

MYRIAM: I wanted to live in a church, when I was a kid. I don't even believe in God.

HORACE: No?

MYRIAM: No.

HORACE: What do you believe in then?

MYRIAM: I believe in the sublime nature of the universe. I believe there is a pattern woven into the world, but it is cold, indifferent, and achingly beautiful. We are a negligible part of the most complex Persian carpet ever created, but it is unplanned; no one weaves it. It weaves itself. And there it is.

HORACE: That's God.

MYRIAM: No it isn't.

HORACE: OK. Whatever you say. But that's God.

Long pause.

MYRIAM: The way you talk sometimes . . . you're too clever for me. You get me all turned around in my thoughts until I don't know what to think anymore.

HORACE: Good. My evil plan is succeeding.

MYRIAM: What?

HORACE: Stop thinking.

MYRIAM: I can't. It's an ingrained habit. I can't just turn it off and go through life like a cuttlefish, although sometimes I wish I could.

HORACE: Hey don't knock the cuttlefish. The cuttlefish is much brighter than you think.

MYRIAM: Really?

HORACE: They're about as smart as octopi.

MYRIAM: Oh regular Einsteins then.

HORACE: You're telling me you don't know how smart the octopus is?

MYRIAM: How smart is the octopus?

HORACE: Smarter than a penguin, and they're smart enough to play football.

MYRIAM: Horace, do you have malaria? Is your imaginary heart condition acting up? Because you're not making much sense.

HORACE: OK, let me slow it down for you.

MYRIAM: Gee, thanks.

HORACE: Where shall I begin?

MYRIAM: How about with penguins playing football.

HORACE: Yes. Well, there were a bunch of researchers down in the Antarctic who used to go out every morning and throw around a football on the airstrip. And there would be all these penguins around, just checking out the scene, you know. And so one morning the researchers get there late and wouldn't you know it.

MYRIAM: What?

HORACE: Those penguins are out there on the airstrip, separated into two distinct groups. And the groups would run at each other, and some of them would fall down, and the others would wait until their friends got up again, and then they'd run at each other again. Goodness knows what they would have done if they'd had a pigskin.

MYRIAM: Wow. That's really amazing. Where did you get that?

HORACE: I read a book about animal intelligence.

MYRIAM: No kidding.

HORACE: Yes. I have been known to read.

She reacts.

HORACE: Now wait until you hear about the octopus.

MYRIAM: I'll bite.

HORACE: Hey, save it for later . . . Kidding. OK. Octopi. Well they're really smart.

MYRIAM: So I gather.

HORACE: Yes. There was a research facility that had all these tanks with various types of exotic and rare fish in them. And in one tank was an octopus. And every morning the researchers would come in and find some more exotic fish missing. No one could figure out where they were getting to. So they put a video camera in the lab, just to see what was going on. Well sure enough, they got footage of that sneaky octopus using one of his limbs to undo the latch on the top of his tank. At which time he'd haul himself out and across to the next tank, dive in, stuff himself on rare sushi, and then slodge his way back to his own tank again.

MYRIAM: Wow. Who knew?

HORACE: Yeah. Pretty clever.

MYRIAM: No I mean who knew that octopuses "slodge." Is that really the term they use? Is that a scientific description of the movement?

HORACE: It's more onomatopoeic. Slodge. Dontcha think?

MYRIAM: I would have thought it was more of a "slurch," myself.

HORACE: Point taken. Anyway, the point is –

MYRIAM: The point is octopi are much cleverer than we give them credit for. But do they make good house pets?

HORACE: Not if they eat all your other pets. However, they can be loyal, and they can be trained to do tricks.

MYRIAM: No kidding.

HORACE: Yup. I heard this other story of an octopus with some small European circus. His trainer taught him to do tricks. And he was really good at it. And then one day the circus went out of business. No one paid too much attention to the animals, just barely fed them and that's it. Anyway, that little octopus would do those tricks over and over in his tank, but there was no one there to see it. No one there to reward him. No one there who cared. Eventually he got so lonely he just stabbed himself with his own beak and died.

MYRIAM: Oh my God.

HORACE: I know.

MYRIAM: That is about the saddest thing I've ever heard.

HORACE: I know.

MYRIAM: Oh my God.

HORACE: Are you crying?

MYRIAM: Don't worry, I'll stop. I just can't help it. Don't pay any attention to me.

HORACE: What? How can I do that? I can't just ignore you.

MYRIAM: Of course you can. What are you doing?

HORACE: Looking for a Kleenex.

MYRIAM: Don't do that!

HORACE: Why not?

MYRIAM: It'll just make it worse.

HORACE: How's that? I'm just trying to help.

MYRIAM: Oh God!

HORACE: What did I do?

MYRIAM: Can't you see, any act of kindness now is going to send me over the edge.

HORACE: Can I give you a hug?

MYRIAM: Don't touch me! Just let me get it out of my system. It'll stop. It's just—it's just a physical reaction.

HORACE: Well, of course it's a physical reaction . . . Everything is, isn't it? Why do you want it to stop?

MYRIAM: It's embarrassing.

HORACE: It's OK. You're allowed to cry if you want. Cry as much as you want.

Pause as Horace gives her some time. She looks around.

HORACE: I'm sure he's in Octopus Heaven now, where everyone watches him do tricks and all the angels give him treats . . .

Pause.

MYRIAM: Thanks.

HORACE: It's OK. Hey.

MYRIAM: What?

HORACE: Um. I don't mean to make presumptions or anything. But.

MYRIAM: But what?

HORACE: Well. I know it's a sad story. But it's an octopus. I mean, worse things happen all the time. War. Famine. Disease. Homelessness.

MYRIAM: Thanks for making me feel insensitive.

HORACE: No. No, I just mean to point out . . . well. What is it about this little octopus that's getting to you?

MYRIAM: Why should it be anything? I feel sorry for it, that's all. Poor little guy.

HORACE: Yes. But what does it mean to you?

MYRIAM: How do you mean?

HORACE: Personally. This little guy means something to you.

MYRIAM: I don't think it has to–

HORACE: Ah ah ah—no thinking.

MYRIAM: But how–

HORACE: Tell me what you're feeling when you imagine that poor little octopus, doing his little tricks over and over in isolation . . .

Pause.

MYRIAM: I'm going to die alone.

Pause.

HORACE: You're not going to die alone.

MYRIAM: But people do. People do die alone all the time.

HORACE: Yes, but not you. Not you.

MYRIAM: Why not me?

HORACE: Because. Because you, you have so much—light—in you.

Pause.

HORACE: Myriam, I'm serious.

MYRIAM: But what if it's all for nothing?

HORACE: What do you mean?

MYRIAM: You know.

HORACE: No, what?

MYRIAM: Life.

HORACE: Oh, that.

MYRIAM: What if no one cares? What if there really is no God, which there isn't, what does any of it matter? Why do we continue to do our little tricks if there's no one to pay attention, if there's no one who cares? What's the point of it all? Millions of people go about their business, go to school, get married, have careers, have families, and who cares about any of it, really? They'll die alone one day, and so will their future generations, until no one is left to remember what mark, if any, they made. How many people in the world are like that little octopus, and who's around to pay due respect to their pain? Not me. I'm like everyone else. I'm doing my tricks too. Waiting for monkeys to drop on my head so that I can collect data so that maybe some day we might find out what early man ate tens of thousands of years ago. Well who cares? Early man probably cared about a lot of things, but we'll never really know what they were. The person who sits next to you on the bus probably wonders the same thing. Who cares? The pyramids themselves will crumble into dust, and one day the earth will be consumed by the sun. And slowly the universe turns cold and dies too. Who cares?

God, I feel like I'm being swallowed by a huge clay fish.

HORACE: You lost me.

MYRIAM: I saw this National Geographic special once that showed all the beauty of the ocean floor. All the animals down there. And there was a baby shark, just born, swimming along, minding his own business, and suddenly he was swallowed up by this great ugly clay-like thing. Some bottom-dwelling fish thing. And Bam! He was gone. This little shark. And about ten seconds later, Bam! He was spit out by the ugly clay-fish thing, who apparently didn't fancy baby shark steak. And the shark just goes on swimming, enjoying the movement of his own fins, just like nothing's happened. I discovered that day that the world is full of beautiful things that do nothing but devour each other. That is the world. The world is a Beautiful, Terrible place.

HORACE: Exactly.

MYRIAM: But if you know what I'm talking about, then how can you be so calm? How do you keep swimming, knowing what's waiting out there for you at any moment?

HORACE: I don't have all the answers, Myriam. I just don't worry about it as much.

MYRIAM: Oh, wouldn't that be great, just to enjoy the feel of your own fins in the water. But . . .

HORACE: But what?

MYRIAM: I guess I'm scared.

HORACE: Of what?

MYRIAM: Of being swallowed whole.

HORACE: And what's wrong with being swallowed whole?

MYRIAM: Well . . . you lose yourself . . . Isn't that unpleasant?

HORACE: I don't know. Have you ever tried it?

MYRIAM: No.

HORACE: Let go, Myriam. Stop fighting.

MYRIAM: What, just, let myself get gulped up like so much goldfish food?

HORACE: What's the worst thing that happens? Maybe the Universe isn't Apathy. Maybe what you perceive as apathy is really something else. Maybe you accept kindness instead of being suspicious of it. Maybe someone puts a book on your shelf. Maybe someone swallows you whole and you lose yourself . . . Who knows what you find on the other side?

MYRIAM: Exactly. Who knows?

HORACE: Could be a hell of a thing. But you won't know unless you surrender to it.

MYRIAM: You make it sound so easy.

HORACE: It is.

MYRIAM: What on earth do you get out of this? Out of being my spiritual guide in the forest? What are you afraid of? I know exactly what you think about everything, but I don't know how you feel. You're as tightly wound as an artichoke, you know that? What's at the heart of you, Horace? What are you afraid of?

Pause.

HORACE: I don't know. Maybe I am an artichoke. All show and very little substance. Sort of hollow.

MYRIAM: I don't believe that.

HORACE: That's what I like about you! Despite all your talk, you really do have faith. Right down to your bones. That's what I admire about you. You have faith, you just try to talk yourself out of it. But you know what's inside you—because you're down in the swamp, slushing through it. And you're not afraid to test what you find, or to shape it. You unfold like a flower at the slightest warmth. That's wonderful. You're wonderful. You're full of wonder. And maybe I'm hoping that by being around you, some of that wonder will rub off on me.

MYRIAM: "Leap and the net will appear."

HORACE: Leaping takes an act of faith. Faith is what I wish I had. And I can see you over there, on the brink, and I figure if I can just push you far enough, you'll do it. You'll jump. Because you're braver than I am. And if you go over, maybe you'll pull me over with you. But I can't—I can't do it alone.

Pause.

MYRIAM: Where do we start?

HORACE: I don't know.

Pause. MYRIAM pulls the net forward and up, pulling them together. MYRIAM kisses HORACE; a long passionate kiss between them. A monkey falls out of the sky and lands on the ground.

HORACE: Crap!

HORACE and MYRIAM scramble out of the net. HORACE picks up the monkey and checks him over.

MYRIAM: He'll be all right.

HORACE: No broken bones. Breathing's fine. How'd you know?

MYRIAM: The ground is softer than you think. And when you're relaxed, the fall is never as hard as you think it's going to be. Is it?

Sound of monkeys chattering in the trees.

The Beginning

End of play.

Selected Scenes for Scene Study

For the benefit of actors practicing their craft, students studying acting, teachers teaching acting, teachers teaching plays through the performance of scenes: in this section, four scenes have been selected and set apart. All four scenes feature strong, well-articulated characters. All four represent powerful forces in conflict. The requirements for staging these scenes are relatively modest. Three of the scenes provide equal opportunities for males and females, as they feature males and females in conflict: Myriam and Horace, Tough Guy and Abby, Gordon and Sharon. The fourth, is a slightly larger piece with the four men: Robin, Andy, Randall and Stewart.

Selected Scene from *Monkey Business*

Characters

MYRIAM

HORACE

MYRIAM:	Wow. That's really amazing. Where did you get that?
HORACE:	I read a book about animal intelligence.
MYRIAM:	No kidding.
HORACE:	Yes. I have been known to read.

She reacts.

HORACE:	Now wait until you hear about the octopus.
MYRIAM:	I'll bite.
HORACE:	Hey, save it for later . . . Kidding. OK. Octopi. Well they're really smart.
MYRIAM:	So I gather.
HORACE:	Yes. There was a research facility that had all these tanks with various types of exotic and rare fish in them. And in one tank was an octopus. And every morning the researchers would come in and find some more exotic fish missing. No one could figure out where they were getting to. So they put a video camera in the lab, just to see what was going on. Well sure enough, they got footage of that sneaky octopus using one of his limbs to undo the latch on the top of his tank. At which time he'd haul himself out and across to the next tank, dive in, stuff himself on rare sushi, and then slodge his way back to his own tank again.
MYRIAM:	Wow. Who knew?
HORACE:	Yeah. Pretty clever.

MYRIAM: No I mean who knew that octopuses "slodge." Is that really the term they use? Is that a scientific description of the movement?

HORACE: It's more onomatopoeic. Slodge. Dontcha think?

MYRIAM: I would have thought it was more of a "slurch," myself.

HORACE: Point taken. Anyway, the point is –

MYRIAM: The point is octopi are much cleverer than we give them credit for. But do they make good house pets?

HORACE: Not if they eat all your other pets. However, they can be loyal, and they can be trained to do tricks.

MYRIAM: No kidding.

HORACE: Yup. I heard this other story of an octopus with some small European circus. His trainer taught him to do tricks. And he was really good at it. And then one day the circus went out of business. No one paid too much attention to the animals, just barely fed them and that's it. Anyway, that little octopus would do those tricks over and over in his tank, but there was no one there to see it. No one there to reward him. No one there who cared. Eventually he got so lonely he just stabbed himself with his own beak and died.

MYRIAM: Oh my God.

HORACE: I know.

MYRIAM: That is about the saddest thing I've ever heard.

HORACE: I know.

MYRIAM: Oh my God.

HORACE: Are you crying?

MYRIAM: Don't worry, I'll stop. I just can't help it. Don't pay any attention to me.

HORACE: What? How can I do that? I can't just ignore you.

MYRIAM: Of course you can. What are you doing?

HORACE: Looking for a Kleenex.

MYRIAM: Don't do that!

HORACE: Why not?

MYRIAM: It'll just make it worse.

HORACE: How's that? I'm just trying to help.

MYRIAM: Oh God!

HORACE: What did I do?

MYRIAM: Can't you see, any act of kindness now is going to send me over the edge.

HORACE: Can I give you a hug?

MYRIAM: Don't touch me! Just let me get it out of my system. It'll stop. It's just—it's just a physical reaction.

HORACE: Well, of course it's a physical reaction . . . Everything is, isn't it? Why do you want it to stop?

MYRIAM: It's embarrassing.

HORACE: It's OK. You're allowed to cry if you want. Cry as much as you want.

Pause as HORACE gives her some time. She looks around.

HORACE: I'm sure he's in Octopus Heaven now, where everyone watches him do tricks and all the angels give him treats.

Selected Scene from *Shopaholic*

Characters:

TOUGH GUY

ABBY

ABBY crosses over, grabs her conditioner, and goes to exit the store. Much madness ensues, as alarms go off, she drops her bags, her arm is pinned behind her back by a large security TOUGH GUY.

TOUGH GUY: Hold it right there lady.

ABBY: What exactly can I do for you?

T. GUY: Empty your bags.

ABBY: Oh! I paid for the conditioner. This is a dumb mix up, you know. Here. Just look at this receipt. See?

T. GUY: We'll see about that. Empty your bags.

ABBY: Are you for serious?

TOUGH GUY continues to look at her.

ABBY: Fine.

ABBY dumps her shopping bag on the floor. ABBY watches TOUGH GUY down on his hands and knees, looking at the contents of the bag, and the receipt.

T. GUY: HA! You already had a bottle of conditioner in this bag. And you only paid for one, and you have two . . . Clearly theft!

ABBY: The conditioner was Two-For-One.

T. GUY: Not.

ABBY: Pardon?

T. GUY: Not.

ABBY: Was too.

T. GUY: Not.

ABBY: Too.

T. GUY: Empty your purse.

ABBY: Not.

Pause. ABBY dumps out her purse.

ABBY: There you have it. Pleased now? My wallet.

ABBY puts the wallet in her pocket.

T. GUY: *(as he examines the contents)* Two tampons. One, two, five
             lipsticks, one lip gloss. Geez. Eight hair clips. One tube
             of hand lotion, empty. Two empty packages of cigarettes,
             one full pack, three lighters, one notebook, three pens
             and a mediaeval mystery novel. Phone bill, LRT receipts,
             Tylenol cold tablets and a condom.

ABBY: Do you want to unwrap the condom or anything or make
             sure I'm not smuggling cocaine in sex things? Go ahead, I
             doubt I'll need it.

T. GUY: Empty your wallet.

ABBY: We've had a nice time, playing empty your bags, while we
             both know I haven't stolen anything. But I know you have
             a sad-sack pathetic life with very little joy, so with great
             pity I have gone along with your ridiculous demands . . .

             No. How do I know you are not going to copy down my
             credit card numbers and memorize my social insurance
             number and steal my identity? Or what if you're a psycho
             killer who just wants my address so you can come and
             kill me at night? You have not made a rational, reasonable
             side of yourself apparent before now.

T. GUY: Are you afraid to open it? Are you hiding more stolen
             merchandise in that wallet?

ABBY: I HAVE NOT STOLEN ANYTHING SINCE GRADE FOUR!

T. GUY: So! You don't deny a pattern of theft in your past!

ABBY: Gummy bears! Once! Jar and all! Once! No pattern!

T. GUY: Look lady, let's just get this all sorted out so we can get on with our lives. I don't like you. I don't like you at all. I don't like you in my store, I don't like you with your stuff spread all over my floor. I don't want you here at all. So let's just get on with this?

ABBY: *(holding out the wallet)* Take it!

TOUGH GUY takes wallet and opens it. Inside are a million cards.

T. GUY: Visa. Amex. Buyers Mart Platinum Card— good choice. MasterCard. Sears, Zellers and the Bay. Safeway, Superstore, Rogers Video. Three frequent coffee cards from three different places— no loyalty these days. Air Miles, bank card, phone card, Alberta health care, birth certificate, library card, Chapters discount card and driver's license.

          So where do we go from here, *(looking at driver's license)* Abigail Adams?

ABBY: I go home, and write a letter to the manager. You go home and think about what else you could do for a living.

T. GUY: I have to choose here. To believe you, or to not believe you. To take your word about the conditioner incident, against my better judgment, or to move into a more serious investigation.

ABBY: Are you insane? What don't you get? I am not a criminal. You are not a cop. I have stolen nothing. You have to let me go. That is the only choice.

T. GUY: I just don't know if I believe you. I may not have proof, but I know a thief in my guts. I see it in the back of your eyes.

ABBY: NUT BAR!!!! Mr. Nut Bar, why don't you call the cashier and find out? I am getting the hell out of here . . . and I am going to complain — a lot.

ABBY has gathered up her belongings, and TOUGH GUY is barring the way.

T. GUY: Abigail, I'm going to let you go today, against my better judgment. I can see that this has frightened you, and that is good. Go now, and know that you are barred from this Buyers Mart for the next twelve months. If I see you here, I'll be forced to remove you from the premises and charge you with trespassing.

ABBY walks away. Twilight Zone music.

Selected Scene from *Borrow Me*

Characters

SHARON

GORDON

SHARON:	So, what happened?
GORDON:	Jenny had too much to drink. Russel's walking her back.
SHARON:	She's very sweet, don't you think, in her own way? And very attractive. A remarkable actress, Russel says. He says he thinks she'll go far, I mean she already has. Ever since school you've represented something of a standard that Russel's felt he's had to live up to.
GORDON:	Really?
SHARON:	Oh yes. He's trying very hard tonight to impress you. With everything he's done, and everything he's got.

SHARON turns back to the table.

SHARON:	Anyway, the food will get cold, we might as well eat. And would you like another drink? Russel has been working so much on the film lately it's nice to have company over. I get lonely since we built this new place. In a way I liked the old house, it's like there's no place for me here. Now, when no one else is with me I feel like I'm the security person hired to make the rounds. Check the corner. Check the hallway. Check the bedrooms—here's your drink—some nights I just *float* around from room to room to room like a ghost, I mean, I might as well be a ghost in my own home . . . boo!

SHARON leans in and kisses GORDON, then stops.

SHARON:	That was nice. Is something wrong?

SHARON kisses GORDON again.

SHARON: Just like old times. What's the matter? You don't have to worry about Russel, you *know* he's involved with Jenny, or someone else, or Jenny *and* someone else. It's hard to keep track. Like I said, it's a very big house and a very big city and most films have very large casts, and he's a very, very active husband and with the guest house and all sometimes it can be kind of like playing the shell game on a very large scale.

GORDON: I know all about that.

SHARON: So whatever we do, won't be—are you all right?

GORDON draws away.

GORDON: I feel a little strange.

SHARON: Strange?

GORDON: Hot. And . . .

SHARON: What?

GORDON glances down.

GORDON: I have an erection.

Slight pause.

SHARON: Good. I mean . . . Then everything's working, normally, right?

SHARON approaches GORDON. He draws back.

GORDON: No.

SHARON: What?

GORDON: No. I'm forgetting, *everything.*

SHARON draws close and puts her arms around GORDON.

SHARON: Well. It seems to be coming back to you.

GORDON: Why I'm here.

SHARON: What?

GORDON: It's very . . . seductive.

SHARON: Good. I want it to be.

SHARON snuggles in.

GORDON: Wait, wait. Sharon. This can't work.

SHARON: It seems to *be* working.

GORDON: I mean. I can't do this with you.

SHARON releases GORDON.

SHARON: I see—

GORDON: —Listen to me, Sharon—

SHARON: —You don't have to explain—

GORDON: This is going to sound, weird, *me* saying this, of all people, but listen. Please. You can do better than this, you *deserve* better than this. You have more dignity than to punish Russel for messing around by sleeping with me—

SHARON grabs GORDON and kisses him again. GORDON retreats. SHARON slaps him.

SHARON: What do I care about your reflections on my dignity? This is humiliating, this, *this* moment is humiliating. If you don't want to . . . if you don't feel you can . . . Fine.

But please, don't *advise* me.

GORDON: *(as though still appreciating the lingering sensation of the slap)* Ow.

175

Selected Scene from *The Wild Guys*

Characters:

ROBIN

ANDY

RANDALL

STEWART

ROBIN: I feel like I've absorbed responsibility for every rotten thing that's ever happened on the planet just because I have a penis. So, I have all these wonderful empathetic talks with women about how men have screwed up the world and . . .

RANDALL: *(at the same time as ROBIN)* They all think you're a wimp.

ROBIN: They all think I'm a wimp. So I go out on a few men's retreats to try and discover what being a modern, responsible man is about and now they're calling me . . .

RANDALL: Anti-feminist.

ROBIN: Anti-feminist. I'm sorry but I read Doris Lessing novels, I go to the feminist film festivals. I would never personally pay a woman less than a man for the same job. I don't tell sexist jokes. I know there's a lot of bad asses out there but I'M NOT ONE OF THEM!!

ANDY: It doesn't have to be so confrontational. Barbara and I have found a balance that works for us.

RANDALL: Oh, Maharishi, please tell us what it is . . .

ANDY: She has an absorbing and fulfilling career. I have an absorbing and fulfilling career.

RANDALL: And you meet in Moose Jaw every six months.

ANDY: It's true we don't see each other as much as we'd like to
            but, it's part of being intellectually active and living a full
            life.

RANDALL: Intellectually active is kind of an understatement, don't
            you think?

ANDY: What do you mean?

RANDALL: The last twenty-four hours have been like you're the
            twelve-year-old and we're the ant farm. I mean, this
            group isn't totally equal, is it? We're not exactly the four
            musketeers. One for all and all for one.

ROBIN: Yeah, Randall's right. We're hangin' out all over the place
            here and you're making notes. I've known you for two
            years and I didn't know you had a wife. You've never
            talked about her.

ANDY: Well, I do have a wife. *(beat)* I have a teenage son as well.

RANDALL: *(surprised)* You have a son? So, you're the absent father that
            Bly talks about. How come you didn't bring your son?

ANDY: He couldn't come.

RANDALL: Why not? What about quality time? How come you
            brought us out here and left your own kid at home?

ANDY: I couldn't bring Danny.

STEWART: Why not?

ANDY: *(big pause)* He's on probation. He's not allowed out of the
            city.

The guys are all a little bit shocked. They pause.

STEWART: What did he do?

ANDY: *(with difficulty)* He vandalized a graveyard. A Jewish
            graveyard. I don't know why. A year in therapy later and I
            still don't know why. Where does that come from? Me? In
            some way I can't understand?

ROBIN: Well, you have your wife. You have each other to lean on.

STEWART: My brother stole a car when he was sixteen and got busted, but he turned out to be a good guy. Who knows why young guys do some of the things they do, eh? Mom and Dad stuck with him and he was OK, you know?

RANDALL: The important thing is there're two of you.

ANDY throws his spear on the fire, walks to the far edge of the stage and turns his back to the others.

ANDY: Did you know that in many primitive tribes, boys are kidnapped by the men of the village at a certain age to symbolize their passage from the world of women to the world of men? Often a physical wound is inflicted to be a constant reminder that the boy is now initiated.

ROBIN: Andy. Come and sit by the fire with us.

ANDY: *(back still to the group)* There are so many literary references. The idea of male initiation is embedded in the collective unconscious . . .

RANDALL: Andy? Don't bullshit us, OK? If you don't want to talk to us, that's all right. But don't bullshit us.

ROBIN: A guy doesn't go out and turn over all these psychological stones for the hell of it. A person searches because they're missing something. Come back to the fire.

ANDY pauses, then comes back to the fire and sits down.

RANDALL: It's not a sin to talk about yourself, Andy.

STEWART: Look, you set up this whole weekend so we could get in touch with our feelings. But, like, you're the only one not doin' it. How come?

ANDY: I don't think I know how.

RANDALL: *(gently)* Yes, you do.

The other guys wait.

ANDY: *(takes a deep breath)* The thing with Danny, it's ruined our marriage. Or our marriage ruined Danny. I don't know which. *(pause)* Barbara's having an affair. She doesn't know that I know. But I do. I don't blame her, really. I understand that she needed someone, I just . . .

STEWART shakes his head and puts a hand on ANDY's shoulder.

STEWART: Oh, man.

ANDY: *(struggling)* There's something . . . *(hand to his chest)* . . . in here. I don't know what, something brooding, dangerous . . . I feel like everything I've done, all these years . . . that it's all been for nothing . . . or worse, much worse . . .

RANDALL: You're pissed off, Andy. Admit it.

ANDY: *(stands up again and begins to pace, angrily)* All right. Yes! I am pissed off! I am . . . *(trembling)* outraged! My son is embracing everything I despise in this world . . . I have this . . . urge, this overwhelming urge to break his rotten neck! And my wife . . . she's abandoned us both, exactly when we needed her most! How could she do such a thing!!?

ANDY grips his spear so fiercely that he may lash out at anything. Suddenly, the rage seems to pass.

ROBIN: Let your anger go.

ANDY: *(shaking his head)* No.

ROBIN: Come on, Andy. Let it out! You're mad as hell, you need to let it out!

ANDY: No. *(gives the spear back to ROBIN)*

ROBIN: But, you need to physicalize your rage . . .

ANDY: No, Robin, I don't. *(more quietly)* I don't need to vent my anger on a bush, or paint my face, or anything else. What I need is time to think. I need to . . . start again somehow. *(shakes his head)* I'm fifty years old and I still don't understand anything. *(beat)* I feel so . . . lost.

179

RANDALL: *(puts his hand on ANDY's other shoulder, says kindly)*
             Well, guess what, brother? We're all hopelessly fucking
             lost. And we always have been. *(big pause)* But there is
             one great satisfaction in all this.

ROBIN: *(breathlessly)* What?

RANDALL: At least we know . . . *(points at STEWART)* IT'S ALL HIS
             FAULT!!!

STEWART is taken aback at first. But RANDALL starts to smile. ANDY and ROBIN start to laugh. Soon they're all laughing.

Sound offstage: the loud rustling in the bushes.

ROBIN: Oh, my God! He's back.

They all leap up and grab their spears. ANDY picks up the drum.

STEWART: Go away!

RANDALL: G'wan. Get outta here, you stupid bear!

ANDY: *(beating the drum in time)* Go bruin go!

They all stop and look at ANDY, a little surprised, then . . .

ALL: Go bruin go! Go bruin go! Go bruin go!!!

They all start leaping around the fire to the beat of the drum, screaming at the top of their lungs and laughing foolishly at each other. "Go bruins go!" becomes a hockey-arena chant.

ALL: Go bruins go! Go bruins go! Go bruins go!

Stage lights go down.

Selected Monologues

Should you ever intend to audition for a play, there are two things you never, ever want to experience. The first is the curiously disconcerting sensation of lining up with the other actors, patiently awaiting your turn to present, hearing others rehearse their audition pieces and then arriving at the horrifying realization that you have selected precisely the same monologue as fifteen other people in the line.

The other situation you fervently wish to avoid is being asked by the person on the other side of the audition desk, "And how does the way you've interpreted this monologue conform to the earlier scenes in the play?"—only to find yourself compelled to confess that you have not actually read the rest of the play. That you plucked your audition piece from a tattered monologue anthology, and have no idea what occurs in the earlier portions of the play.

Even if you may not actually see the director physically strike your name from the call-back list, you will know that this is what he or she is doing, mentally.

It is with the hope that these unpleasant, unnecessary experiences can be deferred indefinitely that the following fresh monologues are compiled and presented.

Enjoy! *And best of luck.*

Selected monologue from *Monkey Business*

MYRIAM: I saw this National Geographic special once that showed all the beauty of the ocean floor. All the animals down there. And there was a baby shark, just born, swimming along, minding his own business, and suddenly he was swallowed up by this great ugly clay-like thing. Some bottom-dwelling fish thing. And Bam! He was gone. This little shark. And about ten seconds later, Bam! He was spit out by the ugly clay-fish thing, who apparently didn't fancy baby shark steak. And the shark just goes on swimming, enjoying the movement of his own fins, just like nothing's happened. I discovered that day that the world is full of beautiful things that do nothing but devour each other. That is the world. The world is a Beautiful, Terrible place.

Selected monologue from *Shopaholic*

ABBY: I was standing with my back against the wall, the wall of the bank, in the mall. And all these people were walking by me, happy people. People with mortgages, and houses and cars and bags. And I felt like I was really not one of them. I felt like I was from another planet. Another planet far, far away, and the mother ship was never coming back.

I couldn't help thinking—Why am I so different from them? Why do they get to have a house and a job and a mortgage and a Mate and matching furniture? I was positively Dickensian in my dejection. I was Little Dorrit. I was Oliver. I am holding out my bowl to the universe and saying – "Please Sir, can I have some more?"

And then I saw her— Linda, the receptionist, who has my old job. The job I had until two years ago, when I got a raise and a bigger title, Administrative Assistant to the Gen X Accounts Marketing Rep. And I happen to know she has a mortgage. And a husband, and a mouthful of straight white teeth. All things I hated in that moment. And she was coming closer and closer and closer, until her big featured face was right up close to mine.

Selected monologue from *Borrow Me*

RUSSEL: There may very well come a day when I *feel* for people and open up and embrace their, you know, humanity. You may be right. And when that day comes, Jenny—shoot me. OK? Just shoot me. I mean, OK, you take this drug thing, eh? The beginnings of my *incipient* cynicism, if you will, all right? It was a very middle-class operation I was running. Three tidy little bungalows with picket fences, basements chock fulla the latest hydroponics equipment, and thousands of these teeny little plants—you know, I believe I even received a government start up grant to finance this initially, as part of an urban renewal thingee. And my clientele were all very proper moms and dads with their own little bungalows—Anyway, I was doing wonderfully, as I'm sure you can imagine, and Gord can attest I threw great parties—*but*—the cops come by one night. Kick the door down. Do I know how deep I am in the blah blah blah? And how long *exactly* have I been illegally blah blah blah blah and I had just better *cooperate* and so on and so forth and ahhhh—

RUSSEL draws a long pull from his drink.

So what did I do? *Gave them their cut,* of course. *(he laughs)* Gave them their cut! That's all they ever wanted. Major epiphany, that. Give everyone their cut, put enough names on a payroll and you can turn the filthiest lucre ivory-snow white. I mean, what are your rum-runners of yesteryear but the corporate models of today, your crack dealers of today but the CEO's of tomorrow. *(takes another drink)* Anyway, it was just grass and the odd bit'a hash. It's like purchasing a starter home. You build up this little nest egg and then you turn it over. I turned it over into the film industry, which, really, apart from being legal bears an uncanny resemblance to selling drugs.

Selected monologue from *The Wild Guys* (condensed)

ROBIN: No kidding. I feel guilty all the time. Especially with women. Starting with my mother. She made me feel guilty for everything. Even the fact that my father wasn't around anymore. I feel guilty when I hear the newest violence against women statistics. I feel guilty about sexism on MTV. I feel guilty about inequality in the workplace. Laundry detergent commercials. The slave-trade of the seventeenth century, the industrial revolution. All the unresolved North American Native land claims, the automobile, PCBs. The pill, breast implants, high-heeled shoes . . .

I feel like I've absorbed responsibility for every rotten thing that's ever happened on the planet just because I have a penis. So, I have all these wonderful empathetic talks with women about how men have screwed up the world . . . They all think I'm a wimp. So I go out on a few men's retreats to try and discover what being a modern, responsible man is about and now they're calling me . . . Anti-feminist. I'm sorry but I read Doris Lessing novels, I go to the feminist film festivals. I would never personally pay a woman less than a man for the same job. I don't tell sexist jokes. I know there's a lot of bad asses out there but I'M NOT ONE OF THEM!!

Acknowledgements

Theatre is such a complicated, rich act of collaboration that at the end of any kind of production, presentation or publication there are always many, many people to thank. I would like to thank The Killam Trusts for their generous support, the very helpful staff at Lunchbox Theatre, Lunchbox Theatre founders Bartley Bard and Margaret Bard for creating Lunchbox Theatre and generating such a warm and generous home for the one-act play, current Lunchbox Artistic Director Rona Waddington for her generous assistance, The University of Calgary's Department of Drama, Anne-Marie Bruzga, Amos Altman for their work reading the texts, and of course, all the actors, directors, designers, technicians, stage hands who assisted in the development of these plays and without whom there would have been no productions.

Biographies

Clem Martini

A professor of the University of Calgary's Drama Department, Clem Martini is also an award-winning playwright, screenwriter, novelist and writer of short fiction. He is a winner of the National Playwriting Competition, a three time recipient of the Alberta Writer's Guild Playwriting Award, and a Governor General Nominee. His published texts include "The Blunt Playwright", "Illegal Entry", "A Three Martini Lunch", "Turnaround", "The Field Mouse Collection", "The Unauthorized Oral History of Theatresports", and his trilogy of novels for young people "Feather and Bone: The Crow Chronicles." He currently sits on the Executive Council of the Playwrights Guild of Canada in the position of Past President.

Nicole Zylstra

Nicole makes her living as a performer and a writer, and makes her home in Calgary. She has written more than 20 plays, and has been commissioned by professional theatres in Calgary and Edmonton, including Vertigo Mystery Theatre where her play "Innocent Blood" made its world premiere. Her play "Monkey Business" (commissioned and produced by Lunchbox Theatre in 2004) was nominated for a Betty Mitchell Award for Best New Play. As a performer, she has performed professionally all across Alberta, and even appeared in a reality show for sketch comics called "Sketch Troop", and performed at Montreal's Just for Laughs comedy festival. She has written several critically praised hit solo shows and performed them across Canada, and is a 7 year veteran of Dirty Laundry: Calgary's Only Completely Live! Completely Improvised! Soap Opera. She is currently a member of the sketch group Obscene But Not Heard.

Andrew Wreggitt and Rebecca Shaw

Andrew Wreggitt is a Gemini Award winning author of over 50 hours of network television drama in Canada including 11 television movies. He has written four plays (with Rebecca Shaw) and is also the author of five books of poetry.

After an extensive career in advertising, Rebecca Shaw began co-writing plays with husband Andrew Wreggitt in 1991. In 1992 they wrote the highly successful "The Wild Guys", which won the National One Act Playwriting Competition and has been a smash hit across North America. Other plays written or co-written by Rebecca include "Ms Lone Pine", "Dunvegan Cross", "Two-Step", "Shrink Rap" and "The Hundredth".

Glenda Stirling

Glenda Stirling is a Calgary-based director, playwright, choreographer and movement instructor. Her plays include "Dark Isle" (The Globe/Curtain Razors), "Flop" (Quest Theatre), "The Longest One Night Stand in History" (Theatre Impossible), "Dig" (Ghost River Theatre), and "Lillibet" (Ship's Company Theatre).